Arrows Words 1

Arrows Words 2

1	2	3	4	5	6	7	8	9	10	11	12	13
14	15	16	17	18	19	20	21	22	23	24	25	26

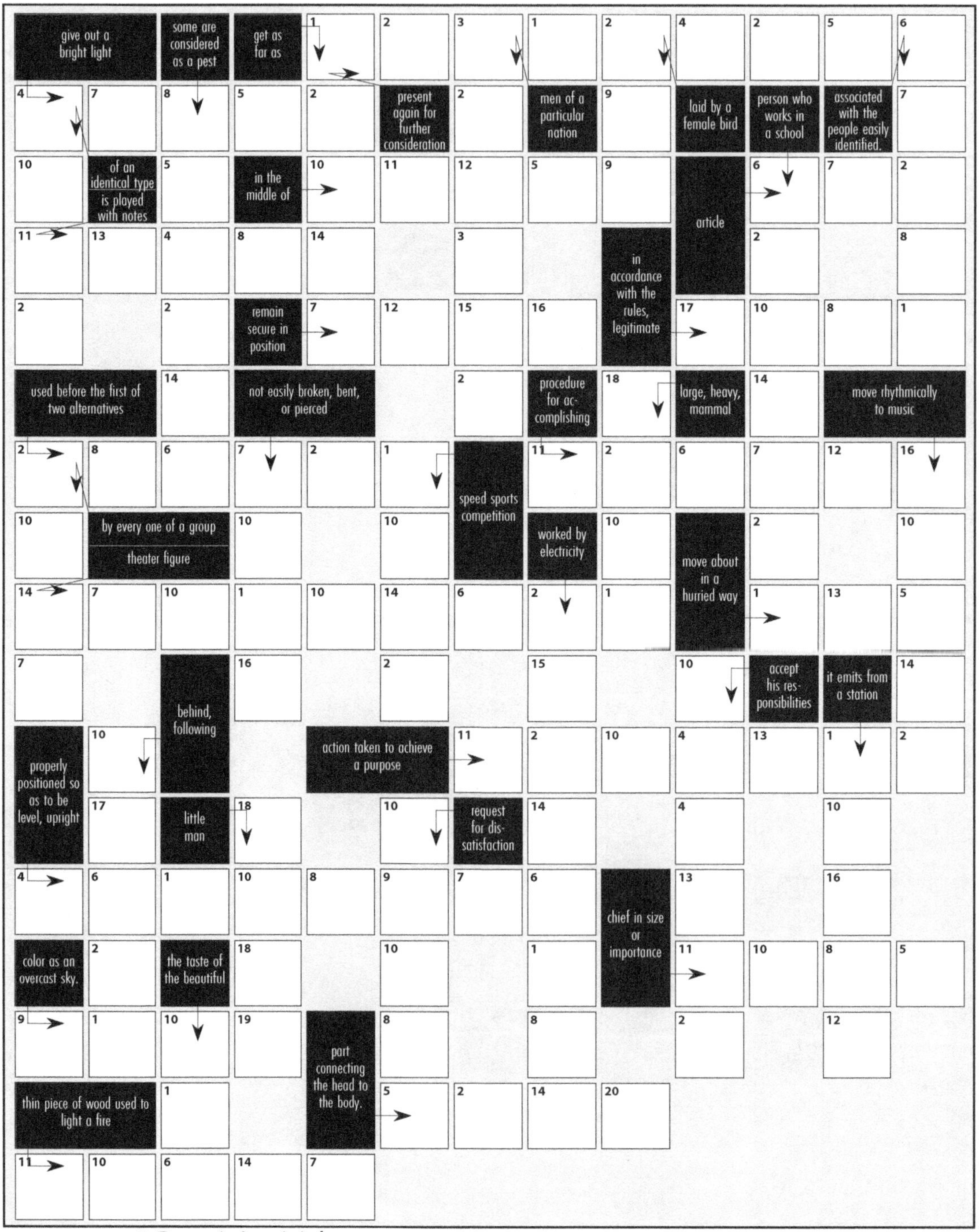

Arrows Words 3

Arrows Words 4

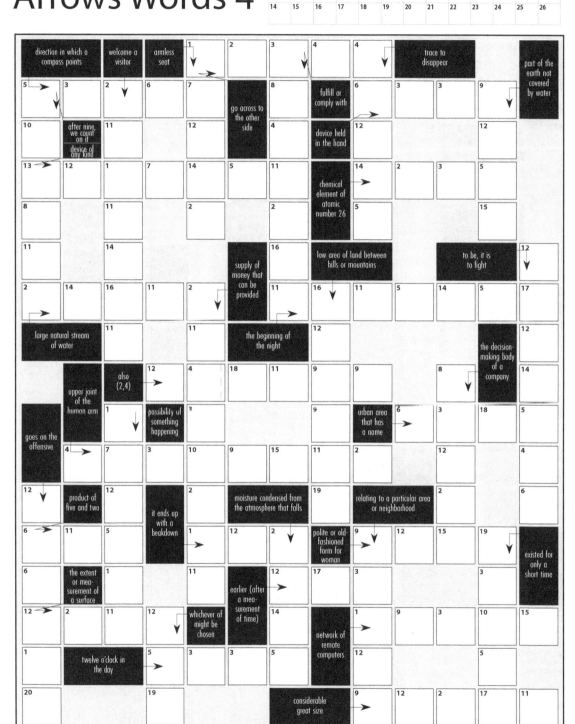

Arrows Words 5

1	2	3	4	5	6	7	8	9	10	11	12	13
14	15	16	17	18	19	20	21	22	23	24	25	26

© Dupuis Logiciels

Arrows Words 7

Arrows Words 8

1	2	3	4	5	6	7	8	9	10	11	12	13
14	15	16	17	18	19	20	21	22	23	24	25	26

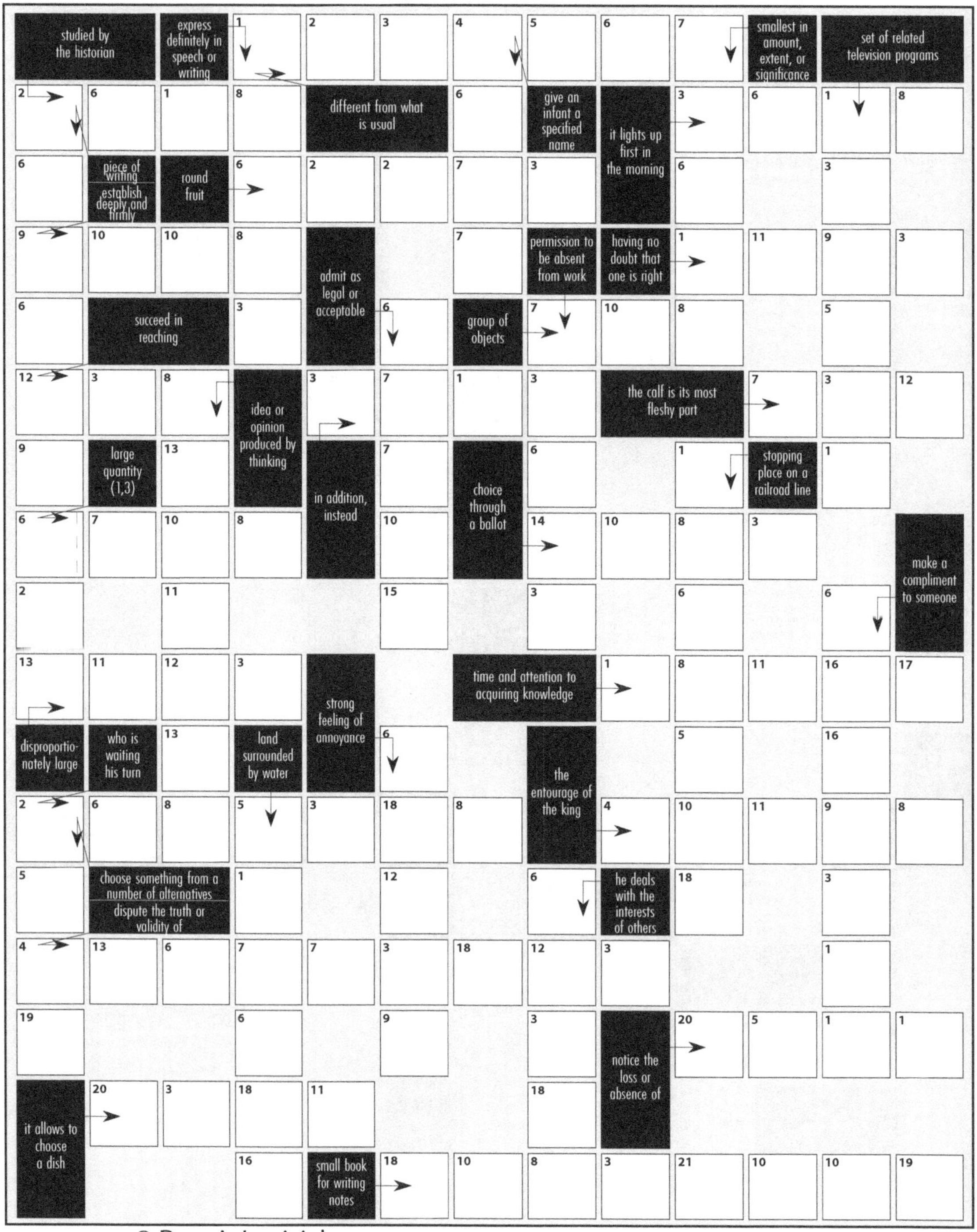

Arrows Words 9

1	2	3	4	5	6	7	8	9	10	11	12	13
14	15	16	17	18	19	20	21	22	23	24	25	26

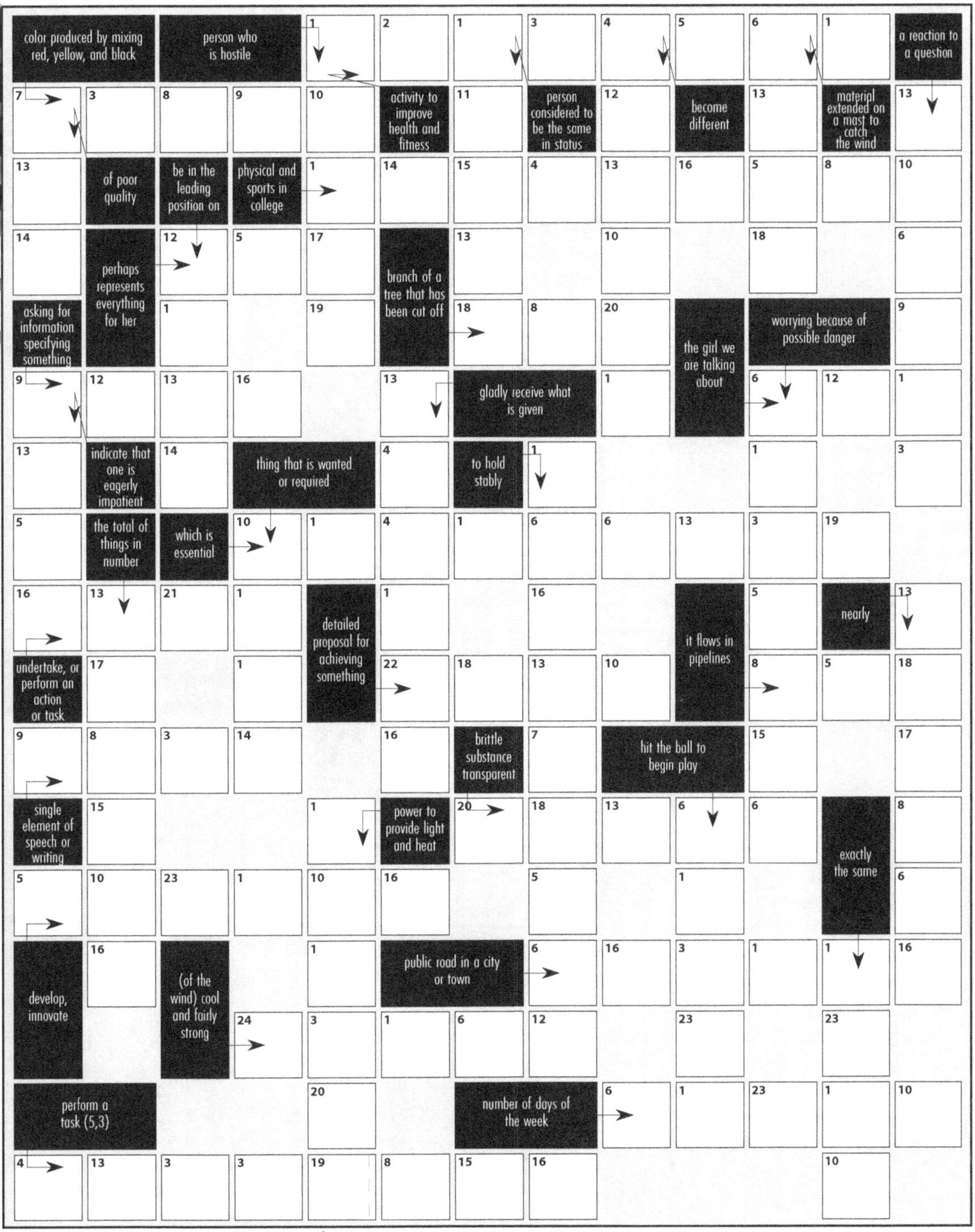

Arrows Words 10

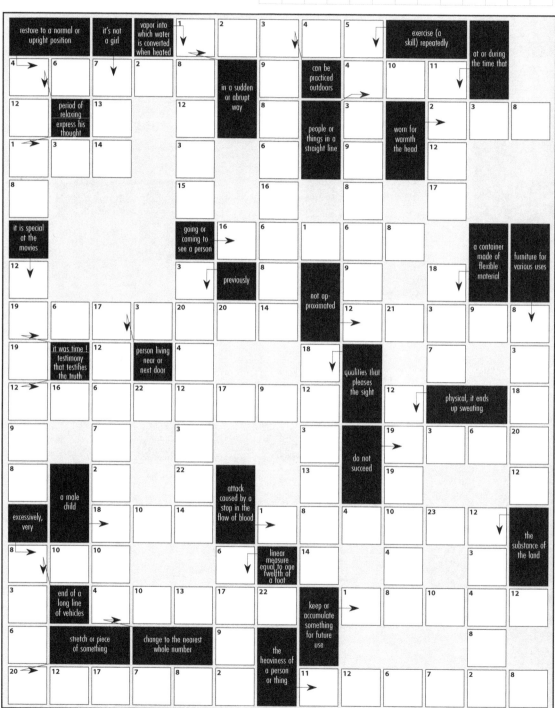

Arrows Words 11

1	2	3	4	5	6	7	8	9	10	11	12	13
14	15	16	17	18	19	20	21	22	23	24	25	26

Clues visible in grid:

- alloy of iron with carbon
- hollow place in a solid surface
- activity done regularly for pleasure
- add salt, herbs, pepper to food
- number of poles
- activity with physical exertion and skill
- take place
- introduces the second element in a comparison
- at any time
- very large expanse of sea
- state of anxiety and uncertainty
- part projecting above the mouth
- only to you
- proposition
- used to express repetition
- teacher of the highest rank
- carrying a weapon
- covering for the foot, typically made of leather
- at the present time
- he gets the rent
- a solid or hollow sphere
- importance, worth of something.
- announce an explanation
- used to refer to two or more people or things previously mentioned
- grow and become more advanced
- information in the form of a graph, or diagram
- group of people with a common interest
- without it, we are not well
- season or preserve with it
- place of management of a company
- exchange something for something else
- number of faces of a dice
- not prevent or forbid

© Dupuis Logiciels

Arrows Words 12

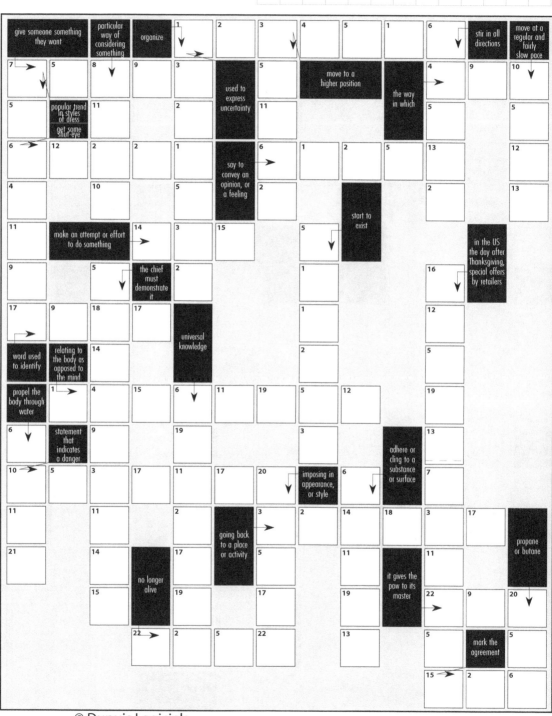

Arrows Words 13

1	2	3	4	5	6	7	8	9	10	11	12	13
14	15	16	17	18	19	20	21	22	23	24	25	26

information acquired by a person

describe the importance of something

it is at the lowest for the sea

give an account in words

after the first in time or order

capital raised by a business through shares.

better to draw the good one

that of the riddle is rarely in the pocket

shed tears

disagreement between two or more groups

armed struggle

make smaller in amount, degree, or size

graduated range of values for measuring

stone structure that divides an area of land

failure of electrical supply

it's not true

situated at a great distance

the way in which one acts

come up by using feet and hands

perceive with the ear

make a sketch

no problem of end of the month

bare or lacking adornment

take something away or off

associated with a female person

large musical instrument having rows of tuned pipes

operate or function, especially properly

having a friendly nature

say again something

repeated decorative design

condition under an agreement is reached

which comes right after

consent to do something

machine that converts power into motion

hard, solid, nonmetallic mineral

Arrows Words 14

Arrows Words 15

1	2	3	4	5	6	7	8	9	10	11	12	13
14	15	16	17	18	19	20	21	22	23	24	25	26

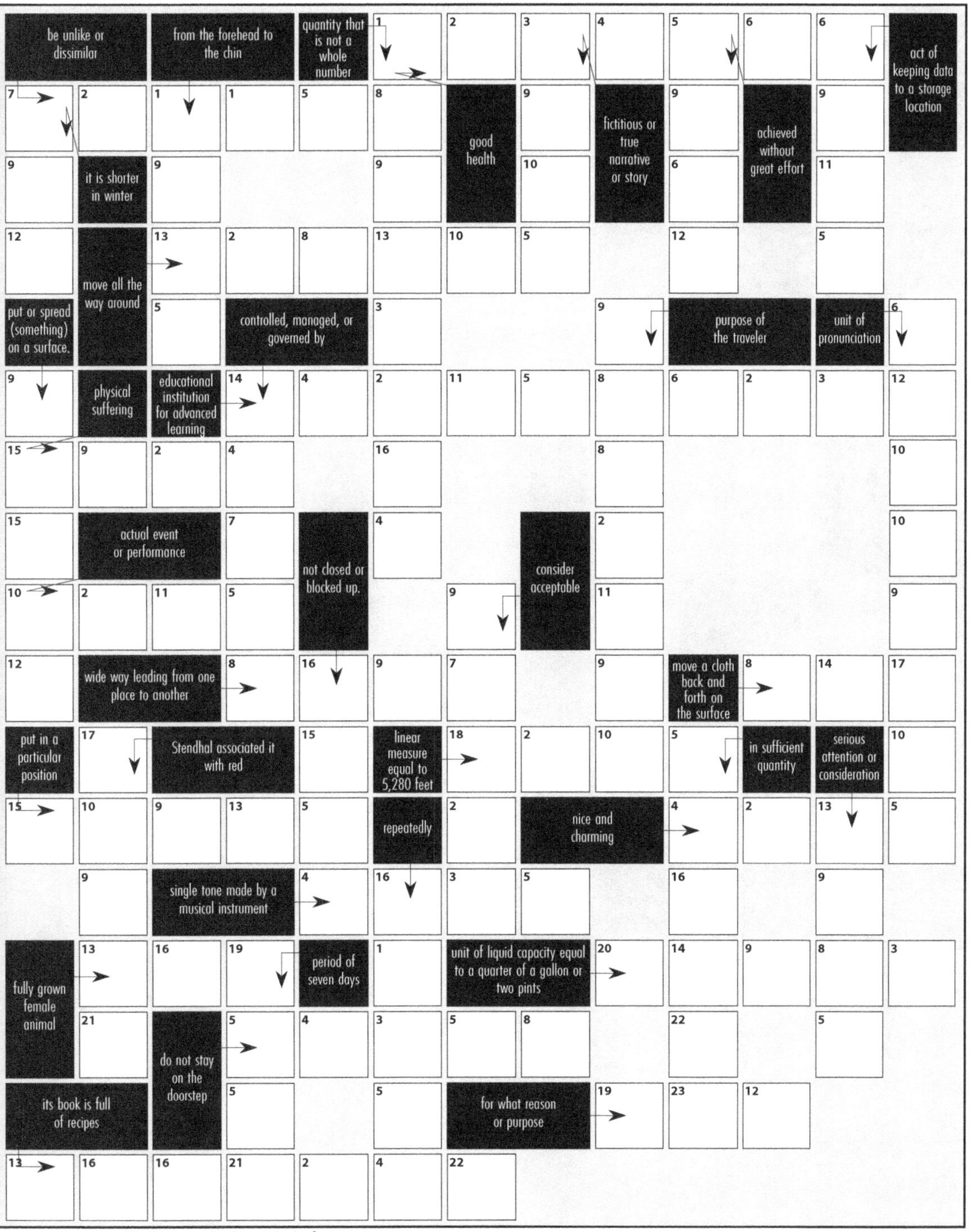

Arrows Words 16

1	2	3	4	5	6	7	8	9	10	11	12	13
14	15	16	17	18	19	20	21	22	23	24	25	26

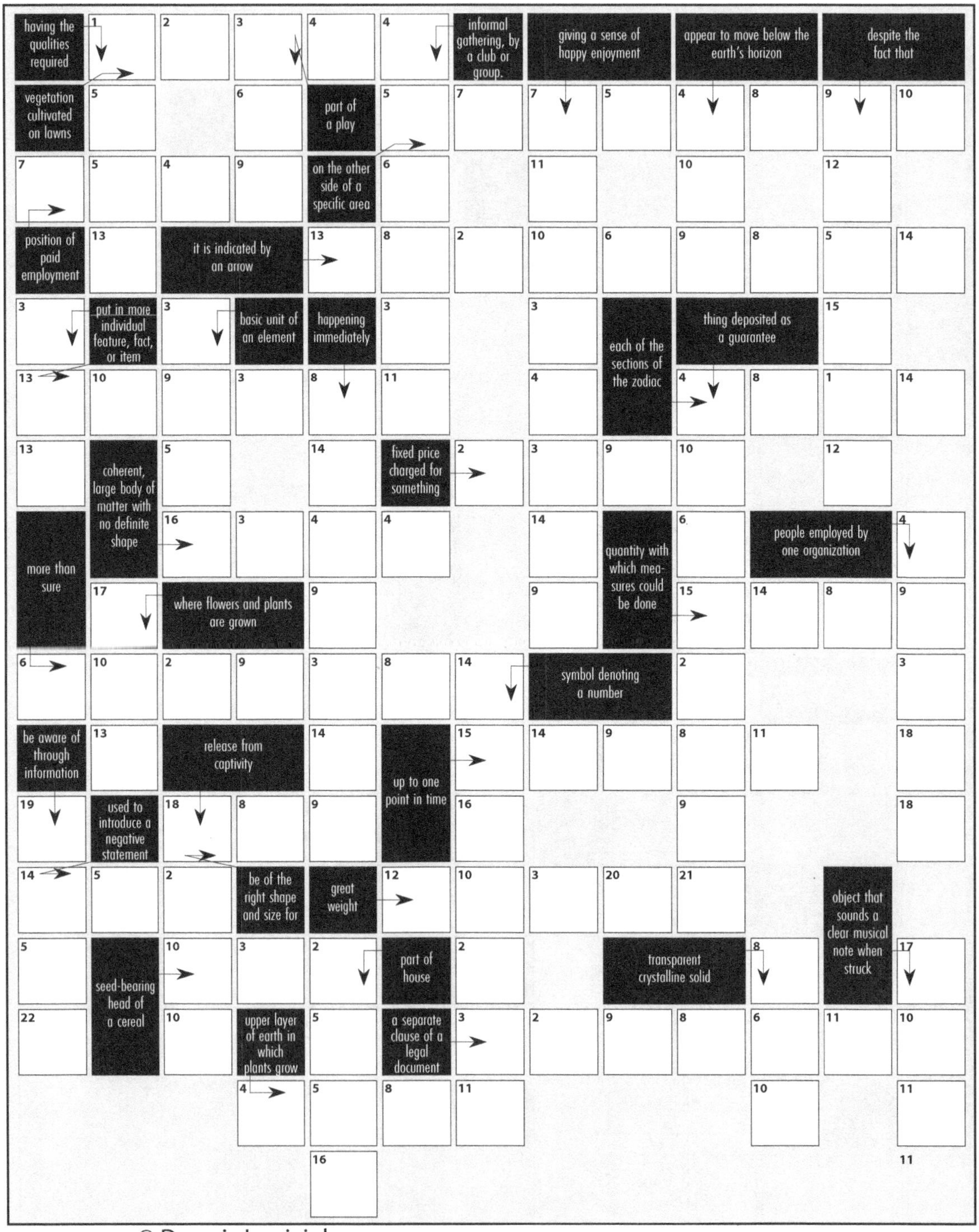

Arrows Words 17

1	2	3	4	5	6	7	8	9	10	11	12	13
14	15	16	17	18	19	20	21	22	23	24	25	26

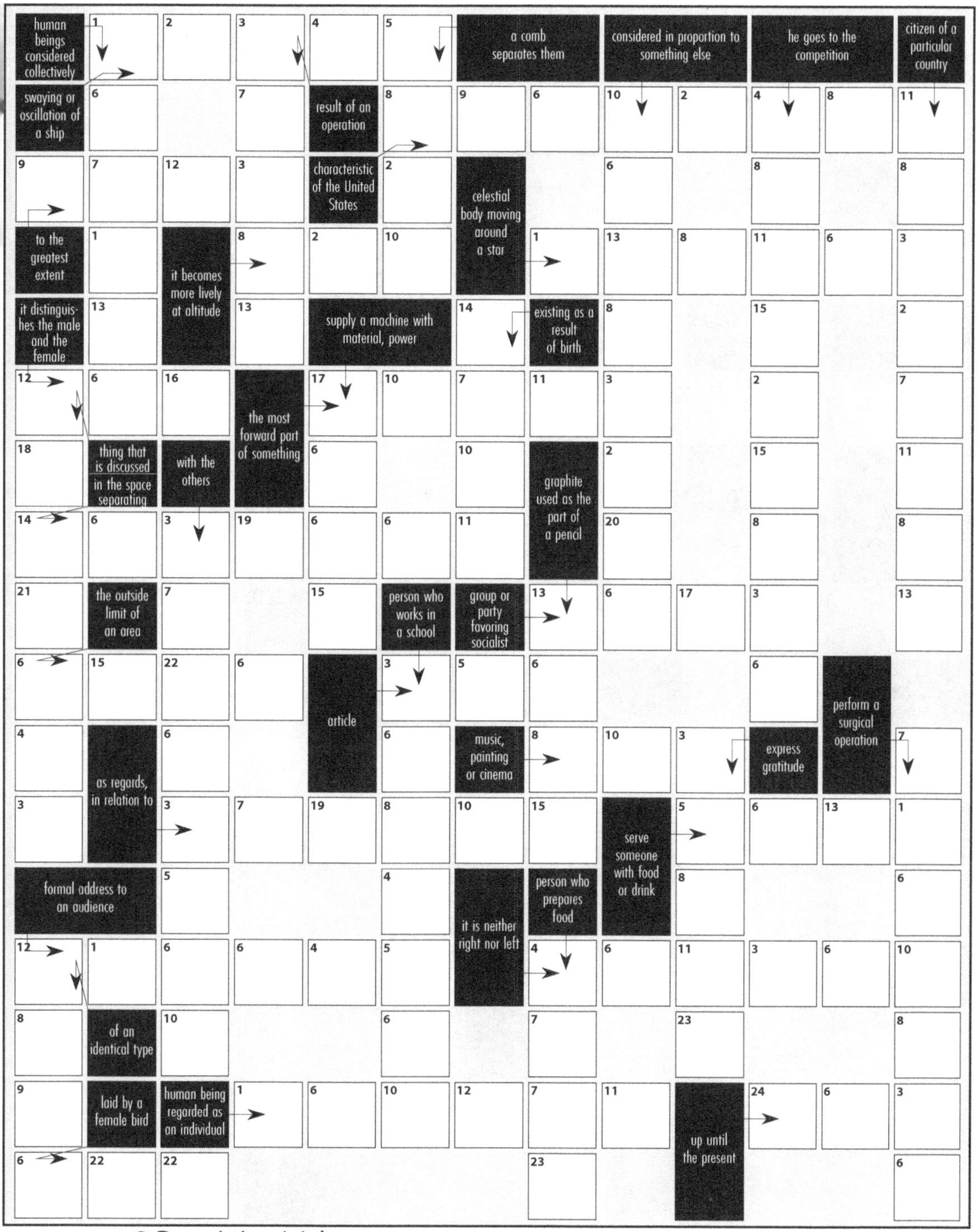

Arrows Words 18

1	2	3	4	5	6	7	8	9	10	11	12	13
14	15	16	17	18	19	20	21	22	23	24	25	26

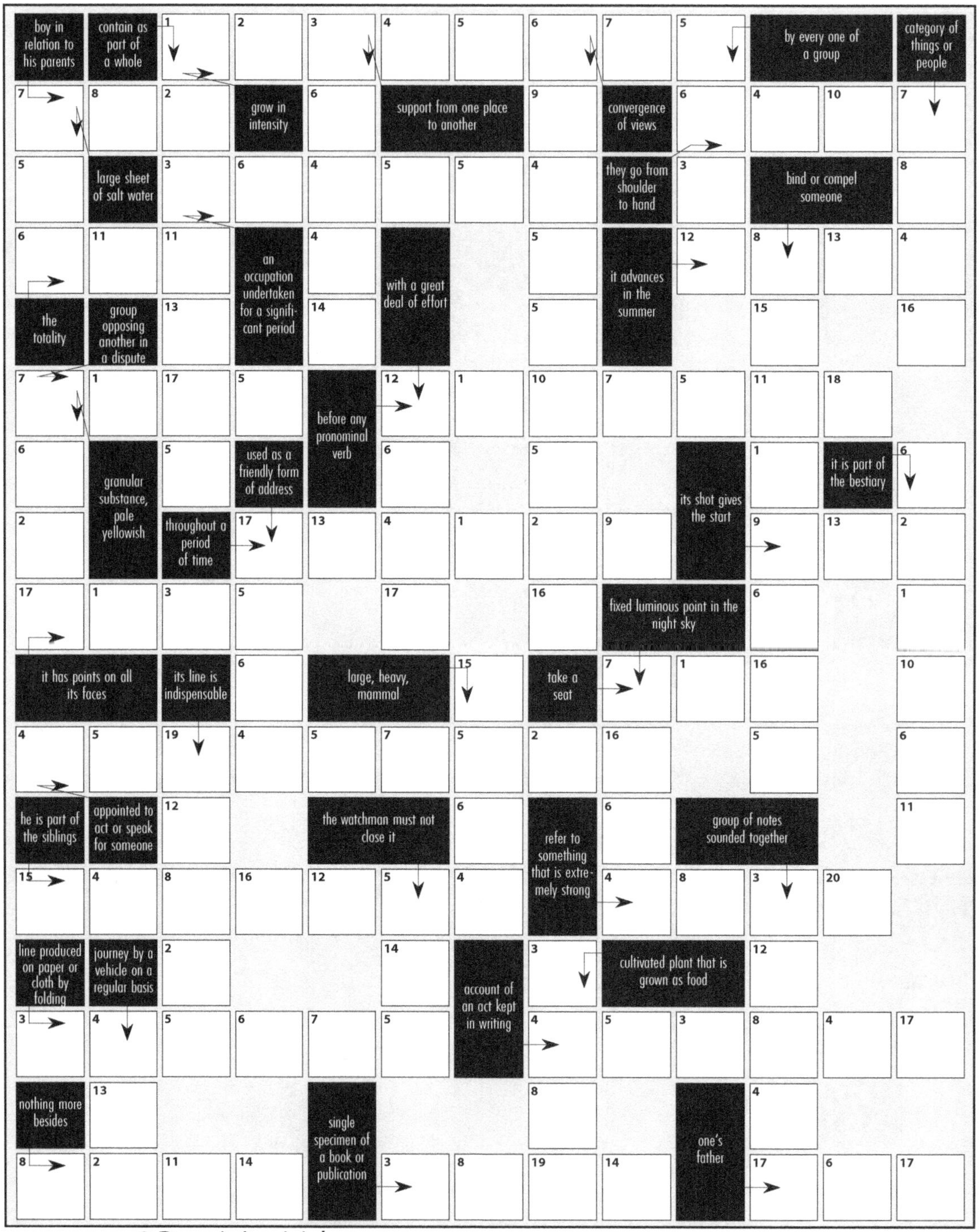

Arrows Words 19

1	2	3	4	5	6	7	8	9	10	11	12	13
14	15	16	17	18	19	20	21	22	23	24	25	26

Arrows Words 20

1	2	3	4	5	6	7	8	9	10	11	12	13
14	15	16	17	18	19	20	21	22	23	24	25	26

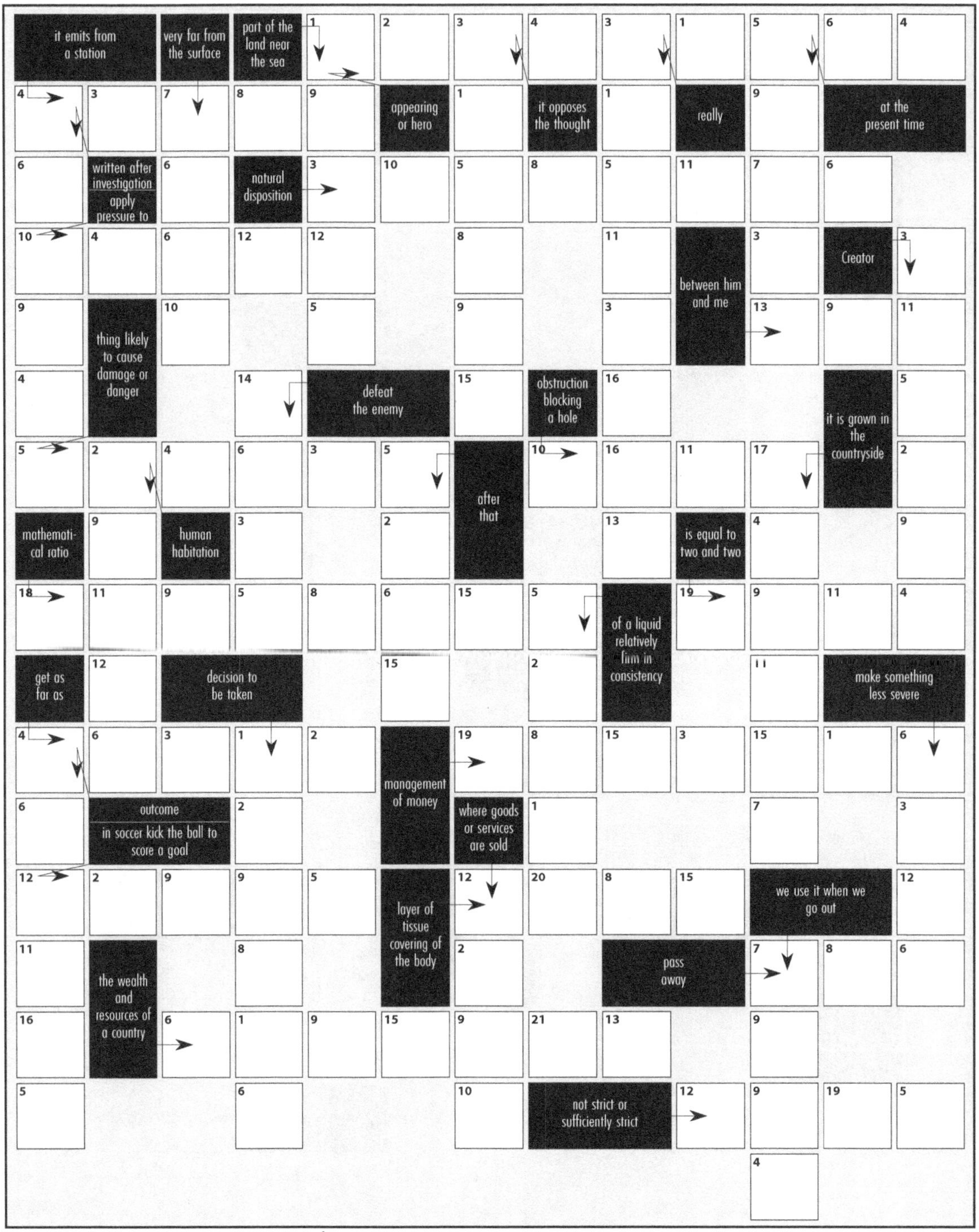

Arrows Words 21

1	2	3	4	5	6	7	8	9	10	11	12	13
14	15	16	17	18	19	20	21	22	23	24	25	26

Arrows Words 22

1	2	3	4	5	6	7	8	9	10	11	12	13
14	15	16	17	18	19	20	21	22	23	24	25	26

Arrows Words 23

1	2	3	4	5	6	7	8	9	10	11	12	13
14	15	16	17	18	19	20	21	22	23	24	25	26

Arrows Words 24

1	2	3	4	5	6	7	8	9	10	11	12	13
14	15	16	17	18	19	20	21	22	23	24	25	26

© Dupuis Logiciels

Arrows Words 25

1	2	3	4	5	6	7	8	9	10	11	12	13
14	15	16	17	18	19	20	21	22	23	24	25	26

© Dupuis Logiciels

Arrows Words 26

Arrows Words 27

Arrows Words 28

1	2	3	4	5	6	7	8	9	10	11	12	13
14	15	16	17	18	19	20	21	22	23	24	25	26

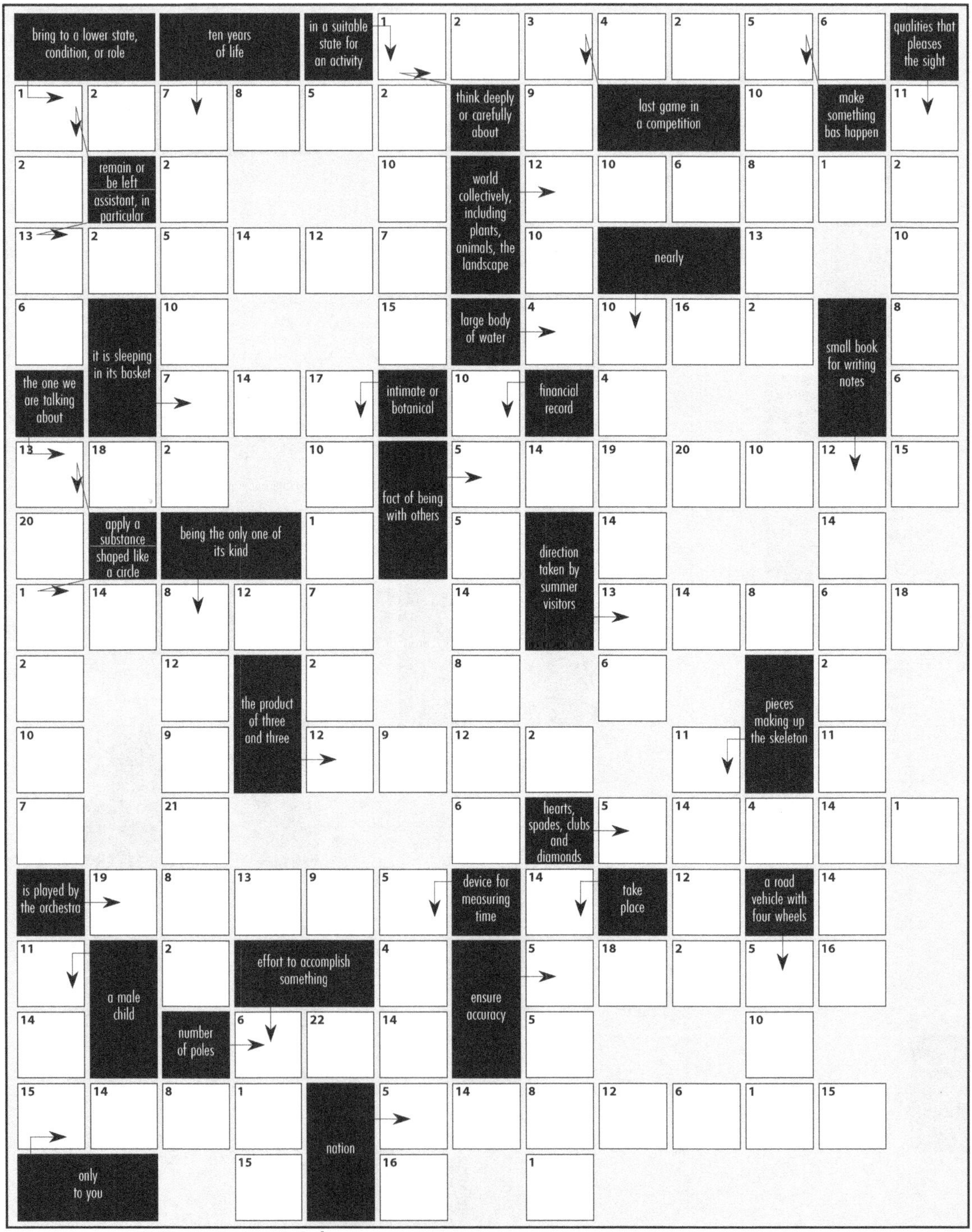

Arrows Words 29

1	2	3	4	5	6	7	8	9	10	11	12	13
14	15	16	17	18	19	20	21	22	23	24	25	26

Arrows Words 30

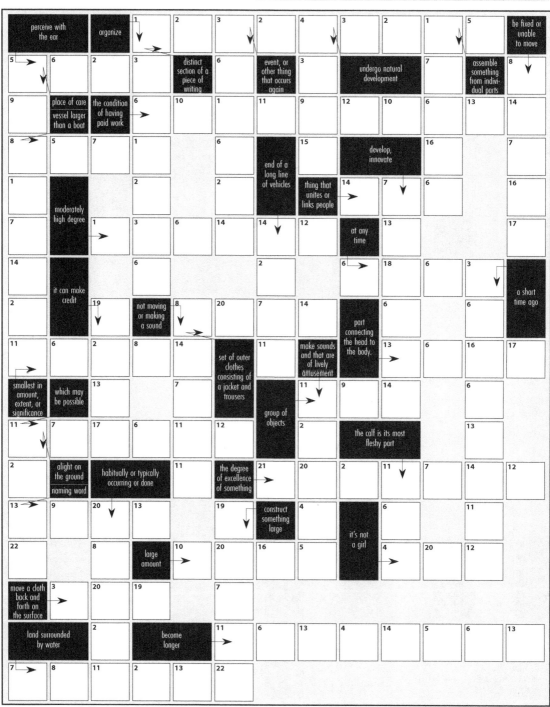

Arrows Words 31

Arrows Words 32

Arrows Words 33

1	2	3	4	5	6	7	8	9	10	11	12	13
14	15	16	17	18	19	20	21	22	23	24	25	26

© Dupuis Logiciels

Arrows Words 34

1	2	3	4	5	6	7	8	9	10	11	12	13
14	15	16	17	18	19	20	21	22	23	24	25	26

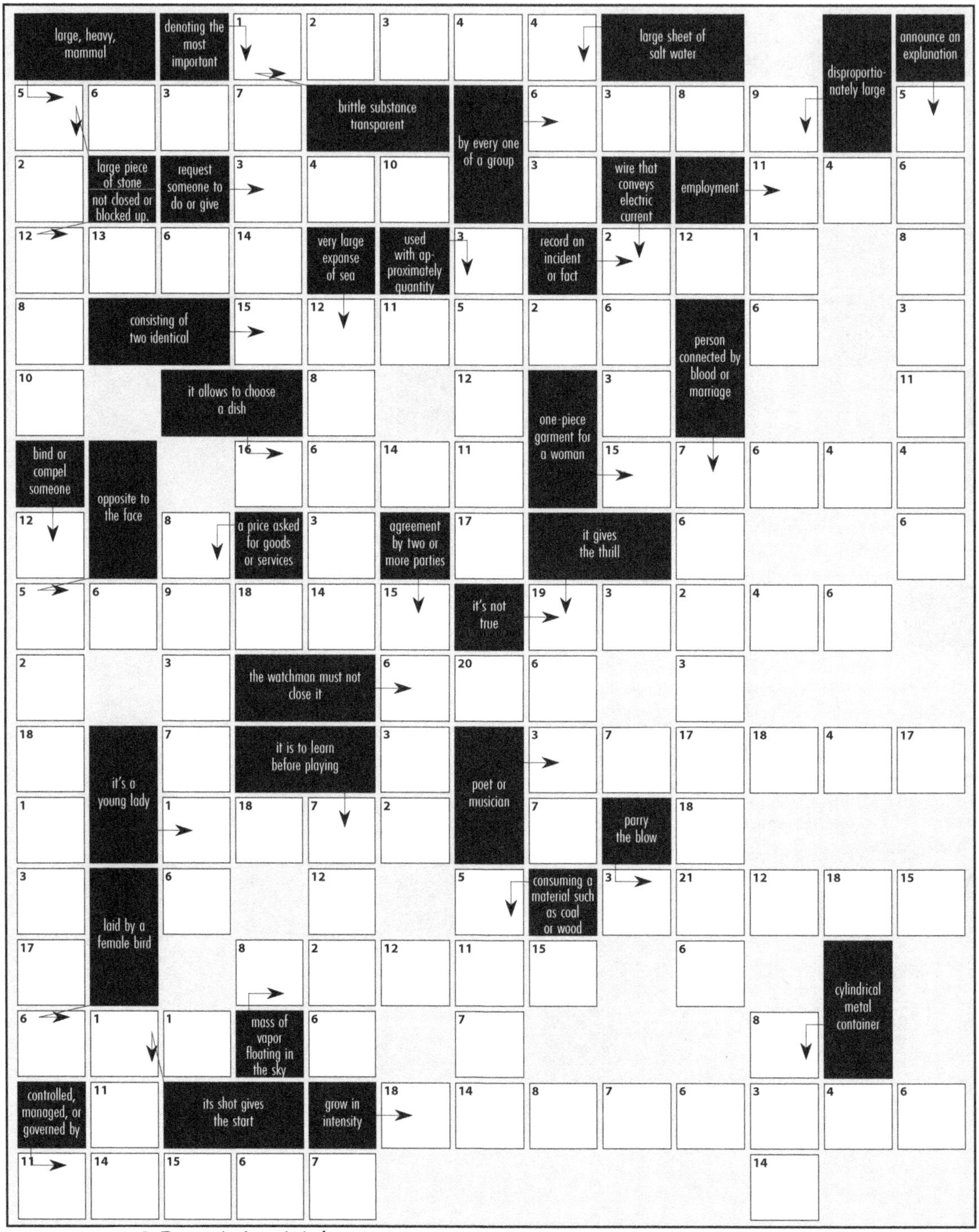

Arrows Words 35

1	2	3	4	5	6	7	8	9	10	11	12	13
14	15	16	17	18	19	20	21	22	23	24	25	26

Arrows Words 36

1	2	3	4	5	6	7	8	9	10	11	12	13
14	15	16	17	18	19	20	21	22	23	24	25	26

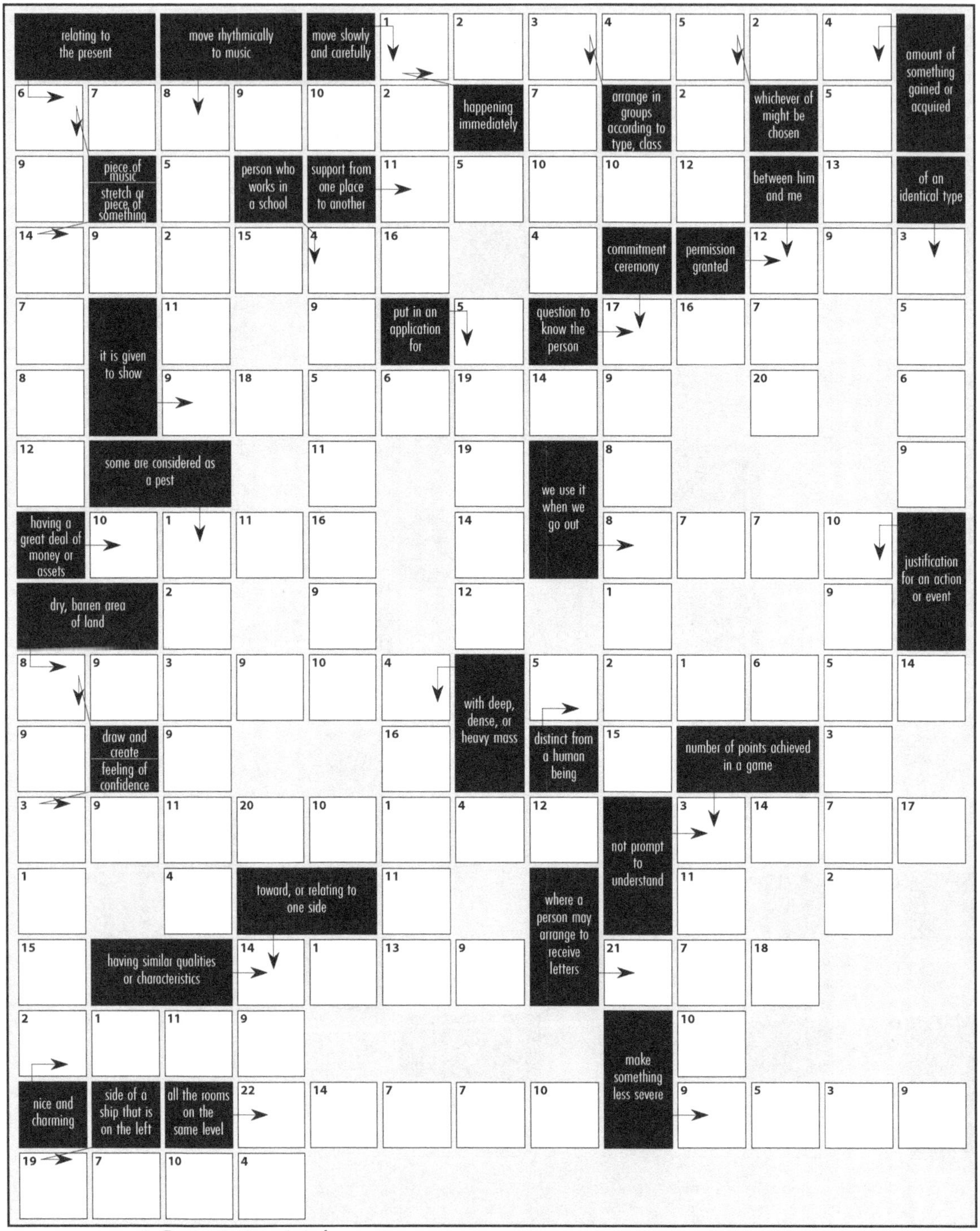

Arrows Words 37

1	2	3	4	5	6	7	8	9	10	11	12	13
14	15	16	17	18	19	20	21	22	23	24	25	26

having the power, skill, means

unit of measure equal to 12 inches

(of the wind) cool and fairly strong

trace to disappear

the wealth and resources of a country

follow as the consequence of something

place to quench your thirst

expanse that is free, available

to be, it is to fight

serious attention or consideration

the reverse of someone or something

earlier (after a measurement of time)

in or after a short time

used for breathing and smelling

easily understood or done

verbal or written answer

activity with physical exertion and skill

suppose without being sure

we stay there when we are sick

he distributes the mail

accept his responsibilities

have a strong effect

contain as part of a whole

coming before all others

young branch springing from a tree

an instance of a disease

situated at a great distance

choose the best or most suitable

part of house

teacher of the highest rank

framework, arrangement of something complex.

people or things in a straight line

possess

Arrows Words 38

1	2	3	4	5	6	7	8	9	10	11	12	13
14	**15**	**16**	**17**	**18**	**19**	**20**	**21**	**22**	**23**	**24**	**25**	**26**

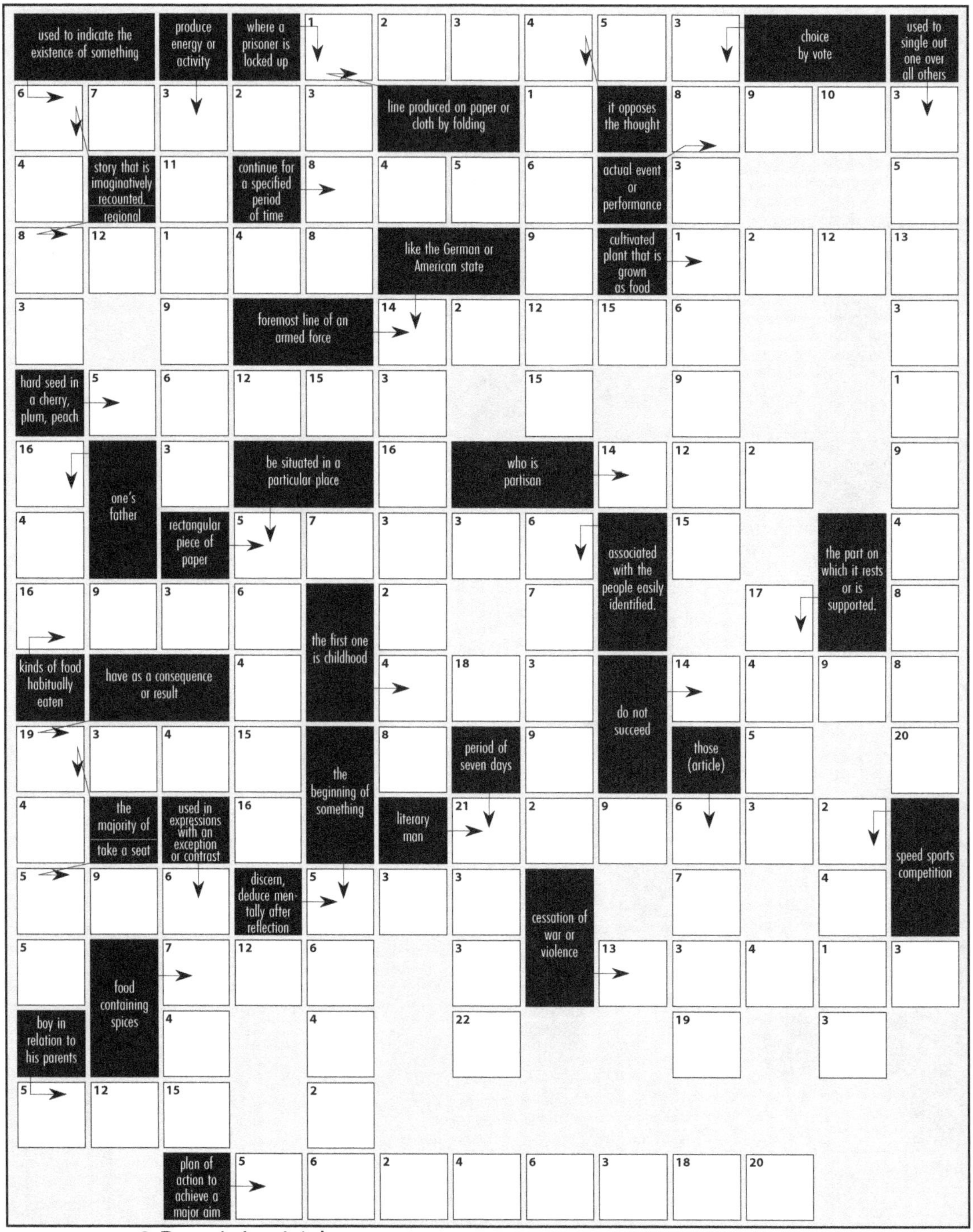

Arrows Words 39

1	2	3	4	5	6	7	8	9	10	11	12	13
14	15	16	17	18	19	20	21	22	23	24	25	26

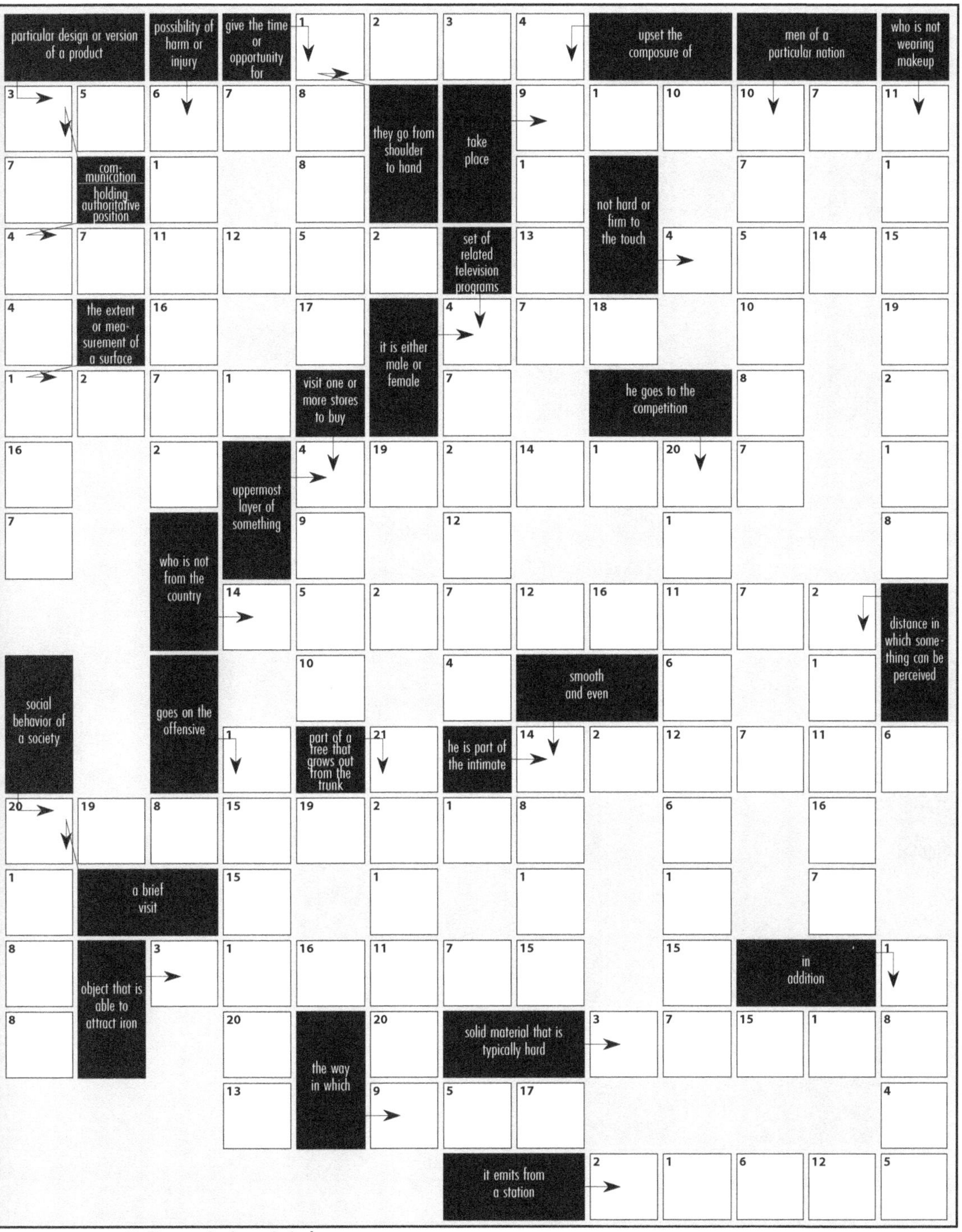

Arrows Words 40

- succeed in reaching
- express definitely in speech or writing
- colored substance that is spread over a surface
- call someone on the telephone
- the ace or the king or the Queen
- cessation of movement or operation
- come near or nearer
- cows floor
- it's a choice
- not us, but them
- worked by electricity
- period when being as a visitor or guest.
- place of management of a company
- he deals with the interests of others
- keep a supply available for sale.
- great weight
- familiar acquiescence
- swallow to feed
- the end of the life
- a device for recording visual images
- at the highest point
- in days gone by
- also (2,4)
- in the middle of
- keep or accumulate something for future use
- which is out of the ordinary
- belonging to or associated with us
- perhaps represents everything for her
- where an incident in life or fiction occurs
- in accordance with fact or reality
- consult it to prepare an itinerary
- series of actions taken to achieve a goal
- official list or register of names

Arrows Words 41

1	2	3	4	5	6	7	8	9	10	11	12	13
14	15	16	17	18	19	20	21	22	23	24	25	26

© Dupuis Logiciels

Arrows Words 42

1	2	3	4	5	6	7	8	9	10	11	12	13
14	15	16	17	18	19	20	21	22	23	24	25	26

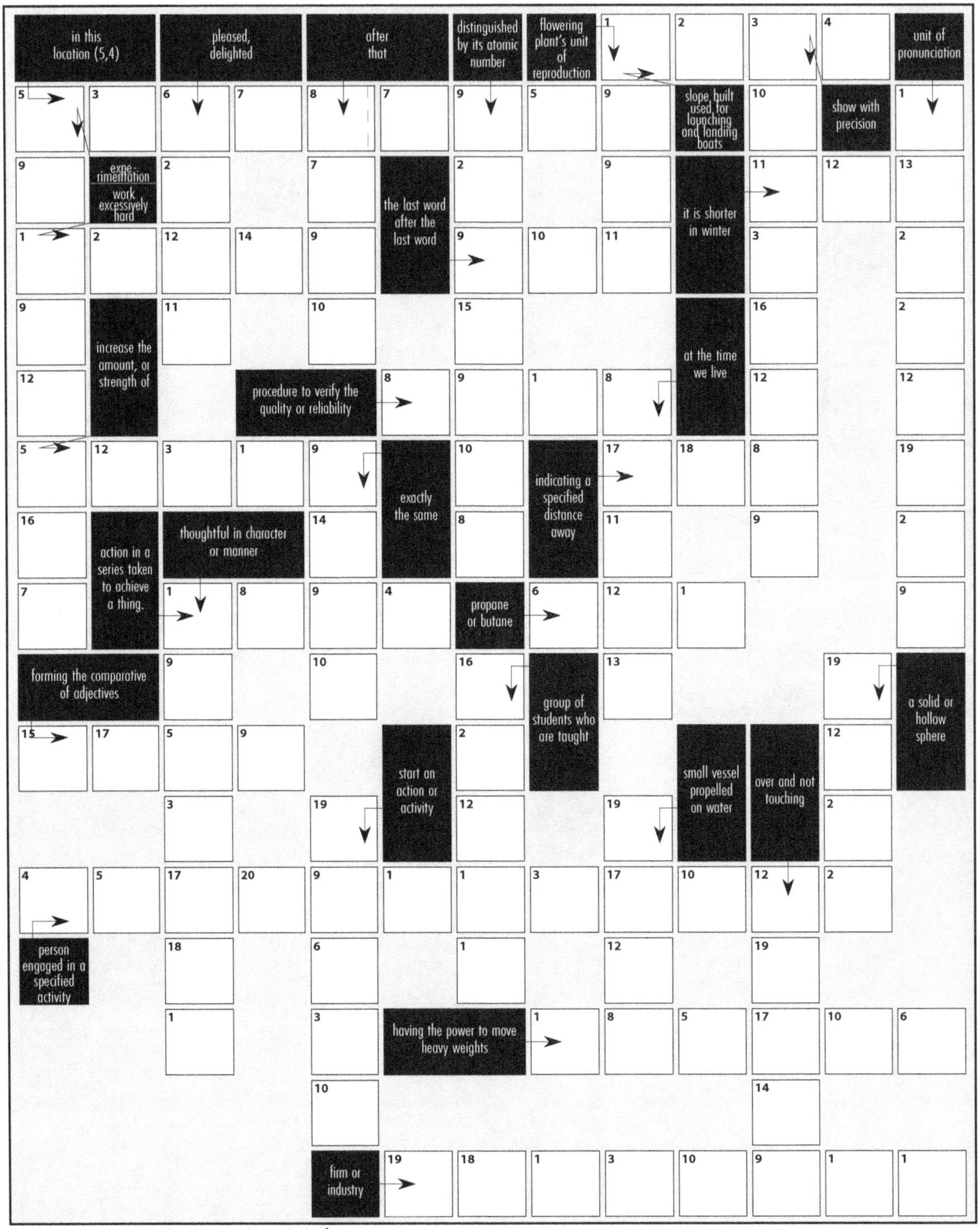

Arrows Words 43

1	2	3	4	5	6	7	8	9	10	11	12	13
14	15	16	17	18	19	20	21	22	23	24	25	26

Arrows Words 44

1	2	3	4	5	6	7	8	9	10	11	12	13
14	15	16	17	18	19	20	21	22	23	24	25	26

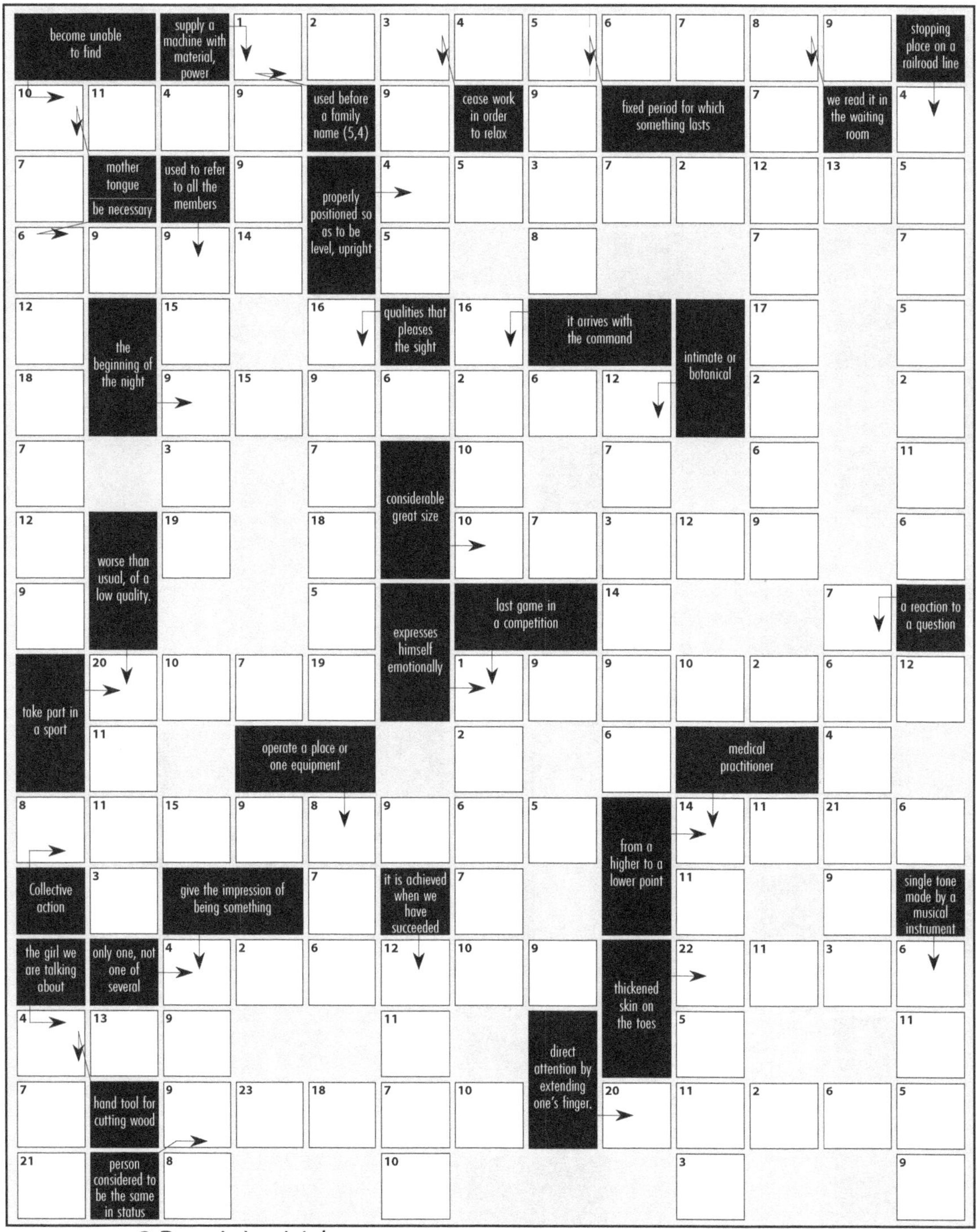

Arrows Words 45

1	2	3	4	5	6	7	8	9	10	11	12	13
14	15	16	17	18	19	20	21	22	23	24	25	26

Arrows Words 46

1	2	3	4	5	6	7	8	9	10	11	12	13
14	15	16	17	18	19	20	21	22	23	24	25	26

Arrows Words 47

1	2	3	4	5	6	7	8	9	10	11	12	13
14	15	16	17	18	19	20	21	22	23	24	25	26

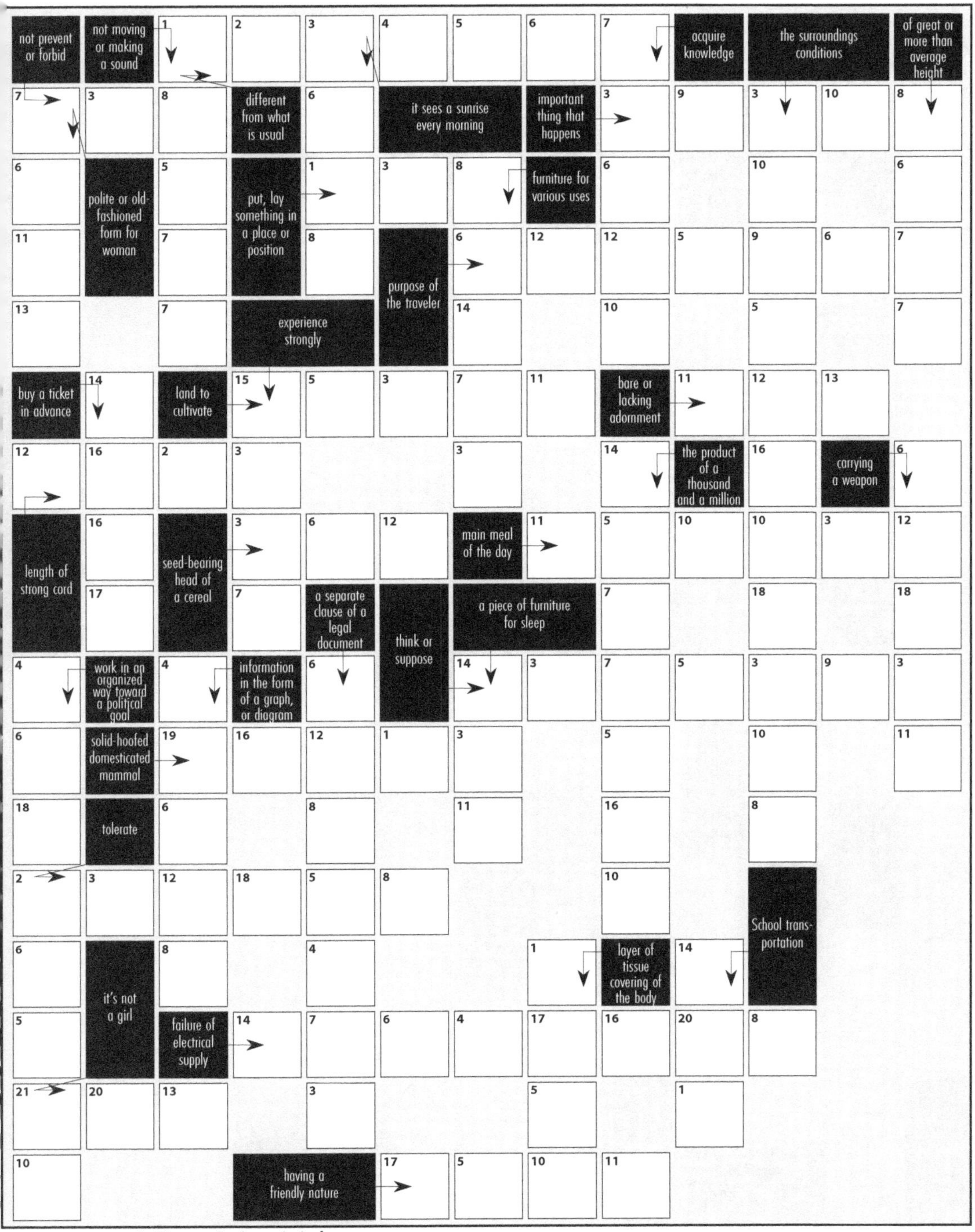

Arrows Words 48

1	2	3	4	5	6	7	8	9	10	11	12	13
14	15	16	17	18	19	20	21	22	23	24	25	26

Arrows Words 49

1	2	3	4	5	6	7	8	9	10	11	12	13
14	15	16	17	18	19	20	21	22	23	24	25	26

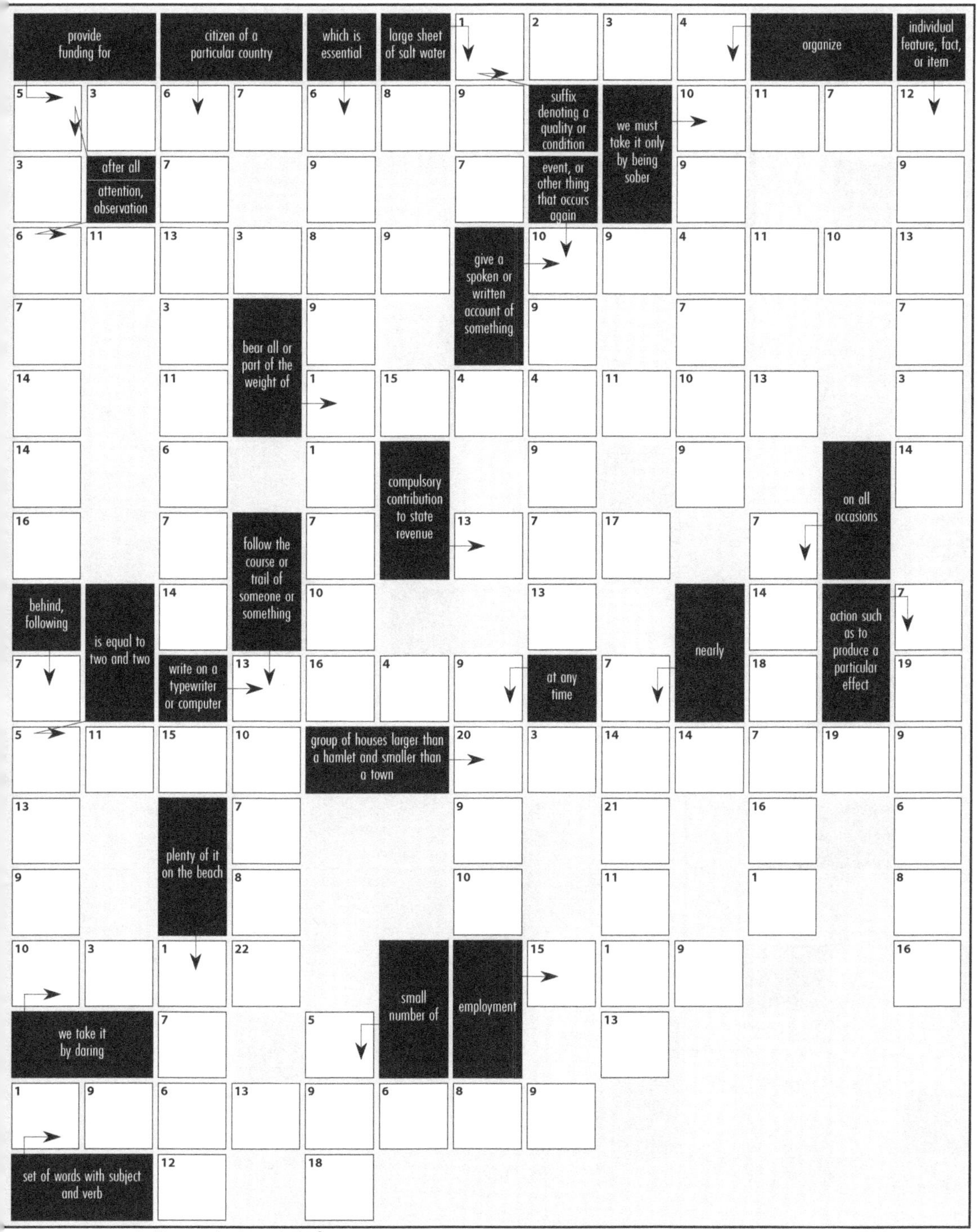

Arrows Words 50

1	2	3	4	5	6	7	8	9	10	11	12	13
14	15	16	17	18	19	20	21	22	23	24	25	26

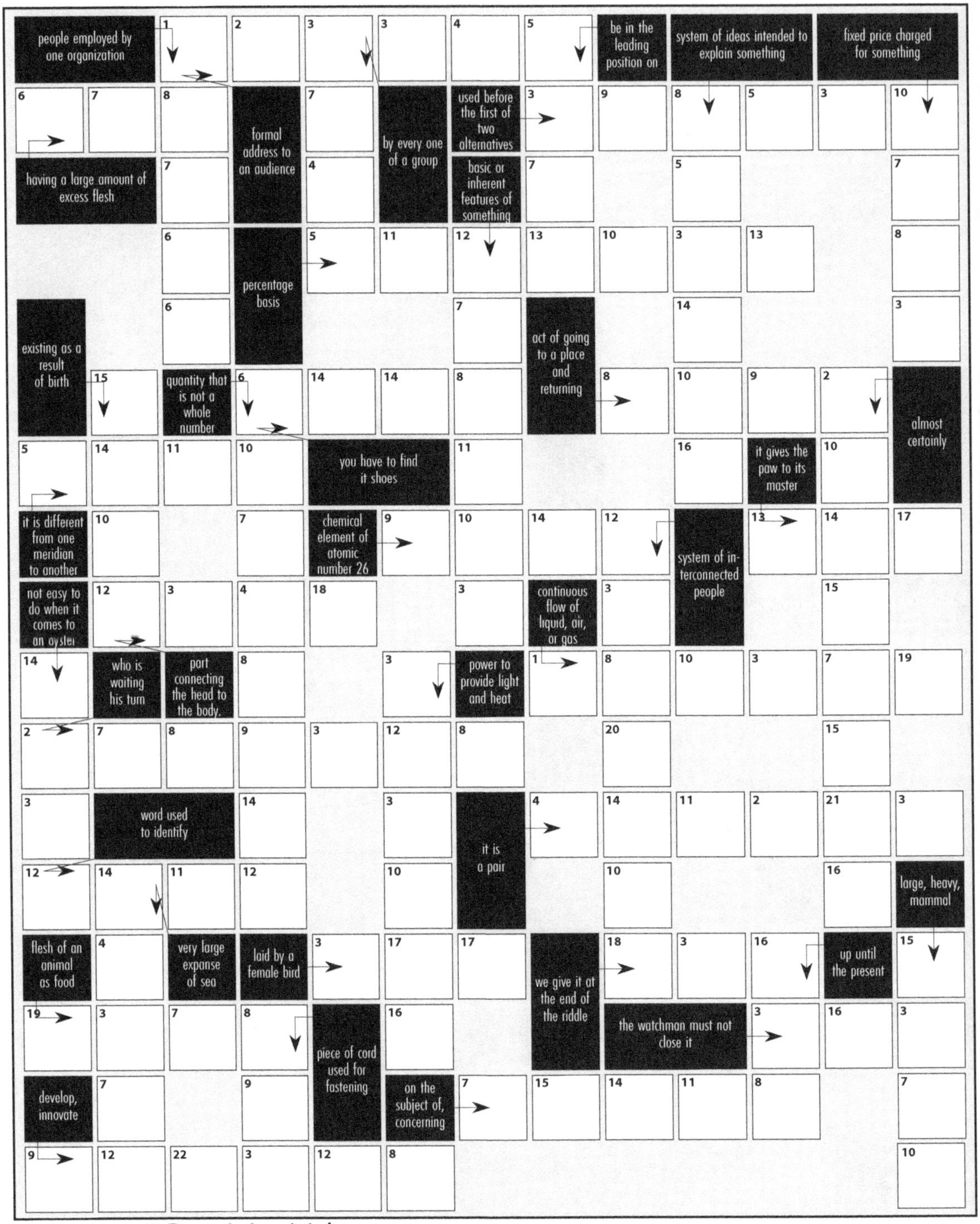

Arrows Words 51

1	2	3	4	5	6	7	8	9	10	11	12	13
14	15	16	17	18	19	20	21	22	23	24	25	26

propel the body through water
colorless, transparent, tasteless liquid
adult human female
carry or bring with one (off)
bring about a problem or difficulty
preferably
good question to know the author
we make some casseroles
admired, or enjoyed by many people
move to a particular position
request someone to do or give
large quantity (1,3)
the condition of having paid work
add salt, herbs, pepper to food
consent to do something
used to refer to a thing, no matter how many
ground adjoining a building or house
make a compliment to someone
it shines in the firmament
controlled, managed, or governed by
move suddenly and quickly
direction followed by a ship, road, or river
put something more
the way in which one acts
reach a place at the end of a journey
associated with a female person
be distant from
move at a regular and fairly slow pace
number of faces of a dice
forms the nucleus of a syllable
clothing for a particular purpose
part of the earth not covered by water
successful result in a contest
pass away
fly without moving the wings
direction in which a compass points

Arrows Words 52

1	2	3	4	5	6	7	8	9	10	11	12	13
14	15	16	17	18	19	20	21	22	23	24	25	26

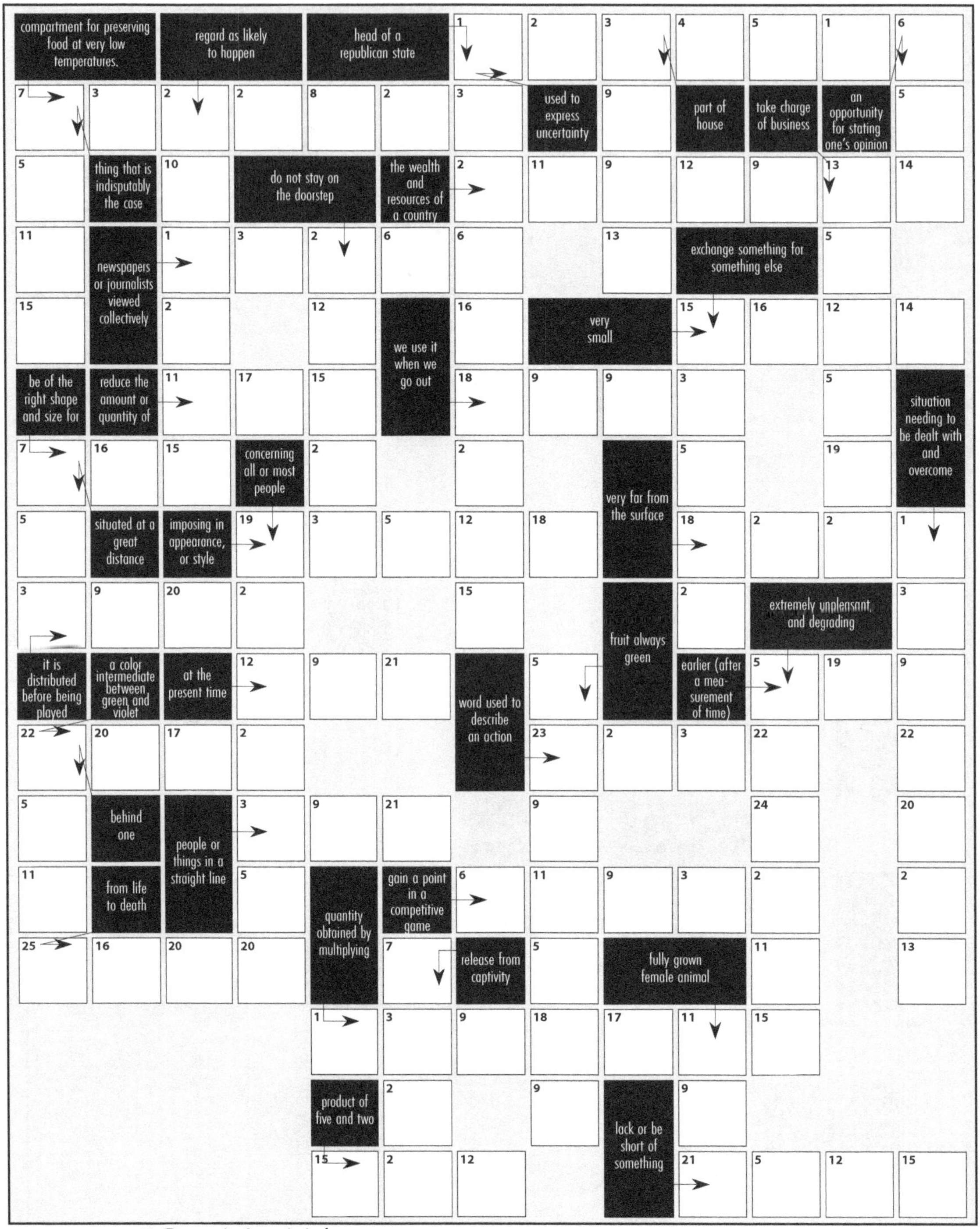

Arrows Words 53

1	2	3	4	5	6	7	8	9	10	11	12	13
14	15	16	17	18	19	20	21	22	23	24	25	26

© Dupuis Logiciels

Arrows Words 54

1	2	3	4	5	6	7	8	9	10	11	12	13
14	15	16	17	18	19	20	21	22	23	24	25	26

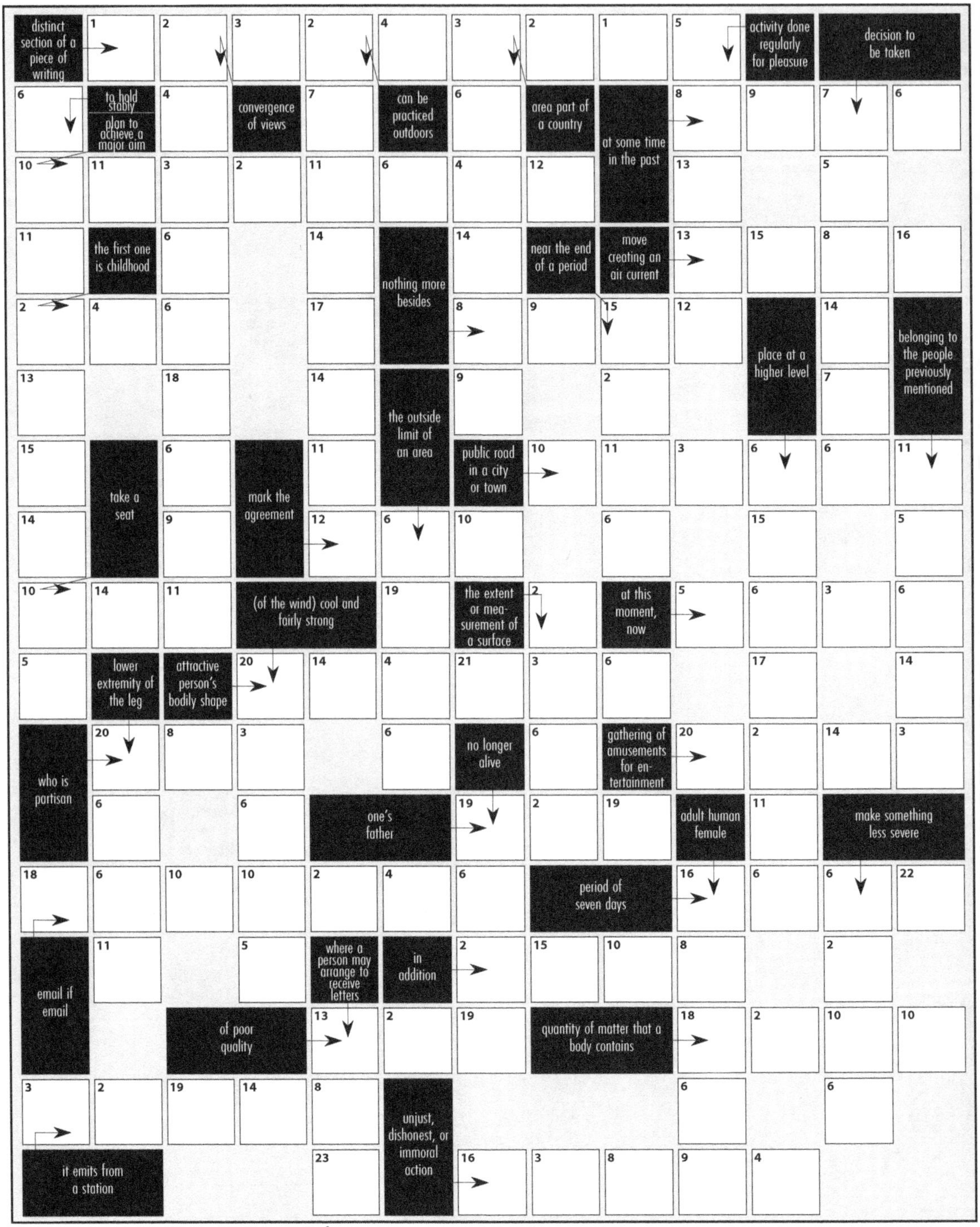

Arrows Words 55

1	2	3	4	5	6	7	8	9	10	11	12	13
14	15	16	17	18	19	20	21	22	23	24	25	26

© Dupuis Logiciels

Arrows Words 56

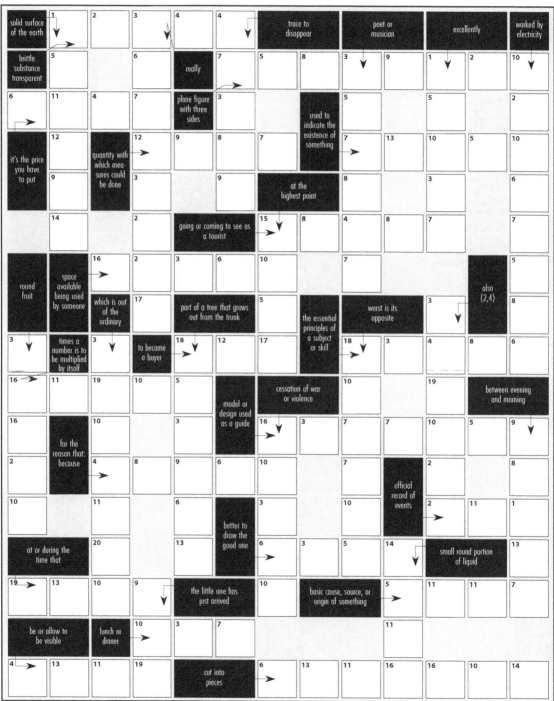

Arrows Words 57

1	2	3	4	5	6	7	8	9	10	11	12	13
14	15	16	17	18	19	20	21	22	23	24	25	26

Arrows Words 58

1	2	3	4	5	6	7	8	9	10	11	12	13
14	15	16	17	18	19	20	21	22	23	24	25	26

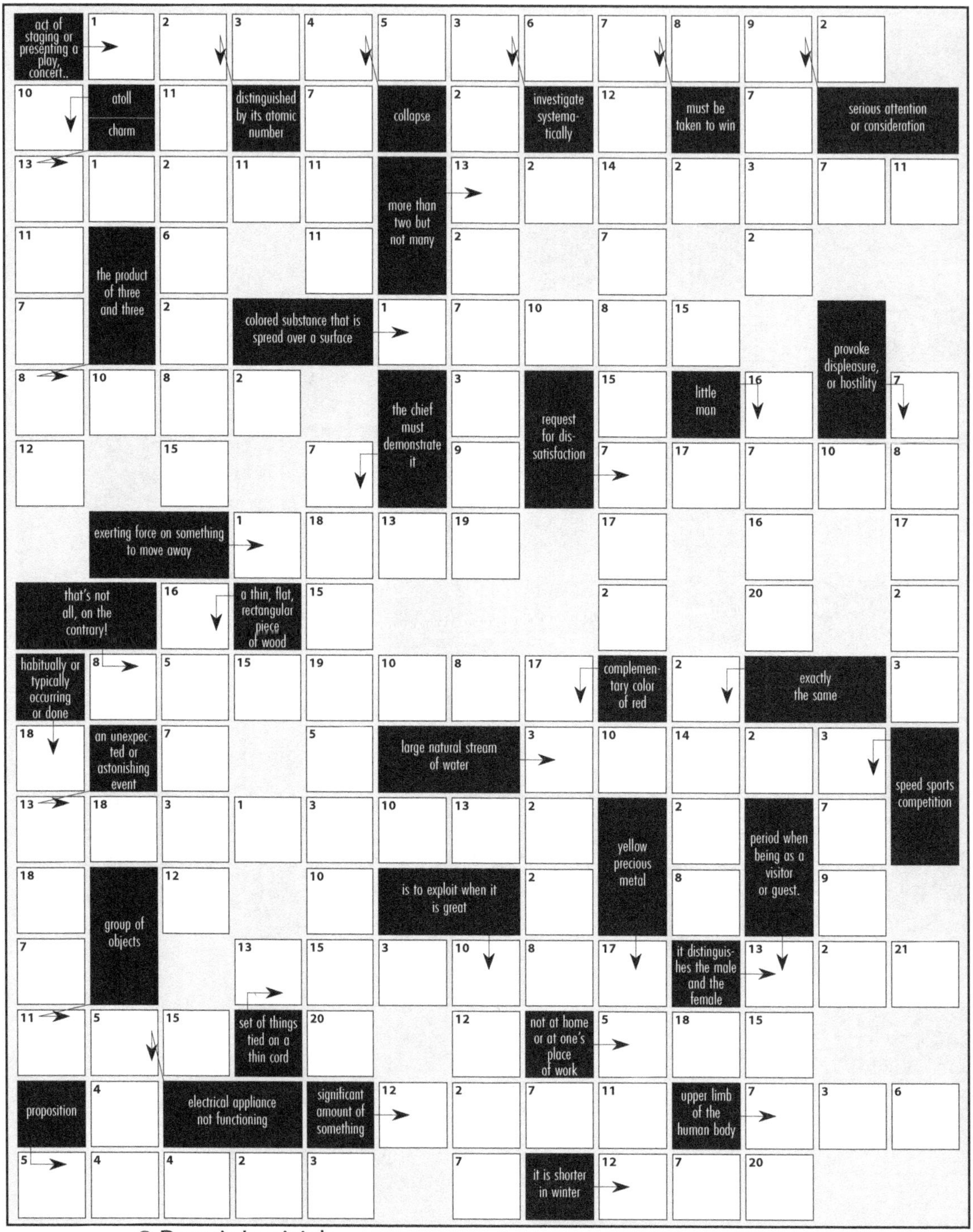

Arrows Words 59

1	2	3	4	5	6	7	8	9	10	11	12	13
14	15	16	17	18	19	20	21	22	23	24	25	26

- the remaining part of something
- be a candidate in an election
- person who is hostile
- give an account in words
- the one we are talking about
- look at written words
- extraterrestrial environment
- having the power, skill, means
- state of lacking basic necessities
- who does not joke
- sit on a horse or a bike
- the moment of the serenade
- notice the loss or absence of
- natural disposition
- body of people with a particular purpose
- come near or nearer
- belonging to or associated with us
- a daily printed publication
- resembling without being identical
- strong enough to withstand adverse conditions
- frequently
- propel a ball with a bat to score runs
- used to refer to two or more people or things previously mentioned
- job, occupation
- being made longer or wider without tearing or breaking
- before the expected time
- group of notes sounded together
- not approximated
- recognize something that is difficult to detect
- on the other side of a specific area
- armed conflict
- differ in size, amount, degree
- action, activity, event, thought

Arrows Words 60

1	2	3	4	5	6	7	8	9	10	11	12	13
14	15	16	17	18	19	20	21	22	23	24	25	26

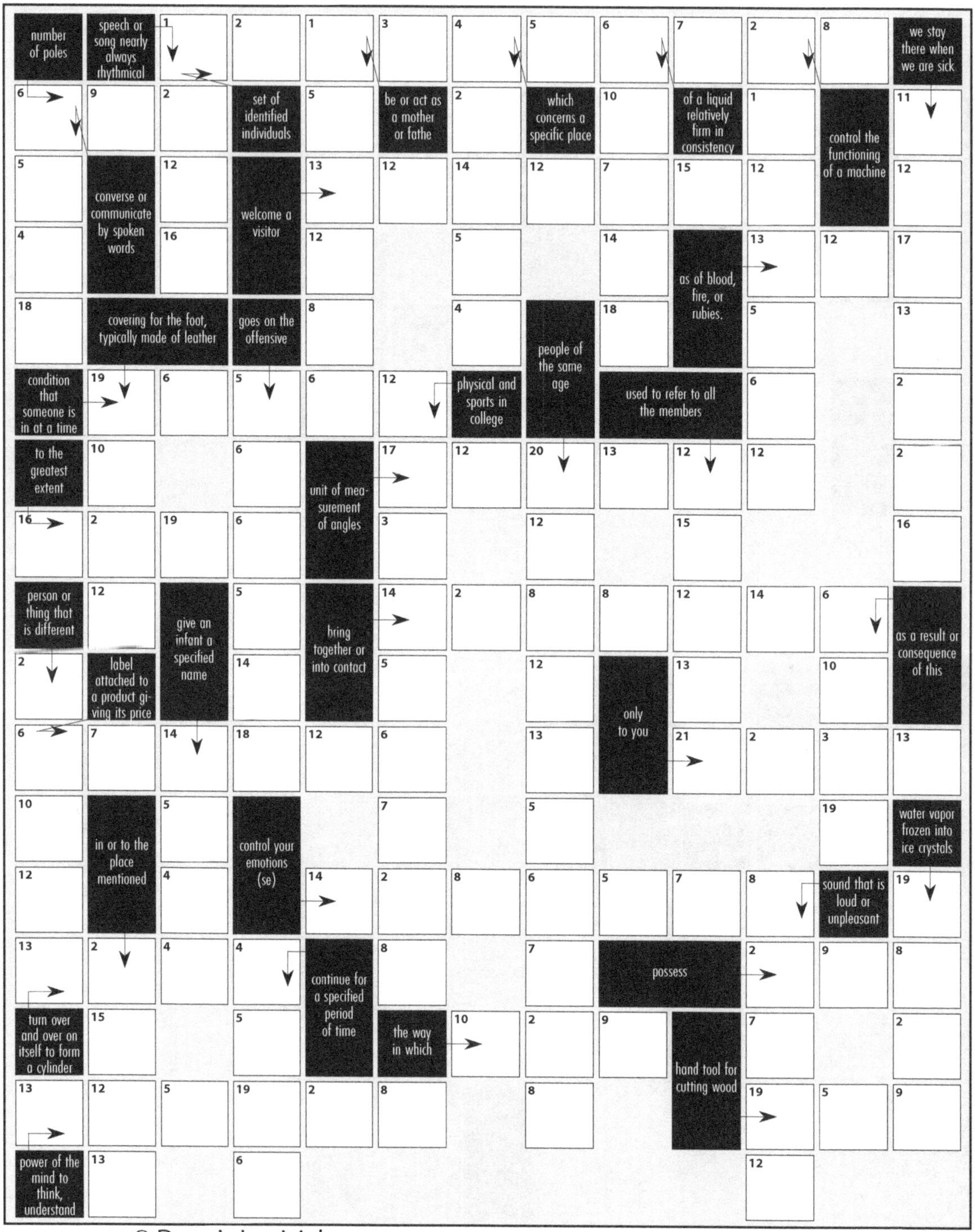

ANSWERS

Arrows Words 1

Arrows Words 2

Arrows Words 3

Arrows Words 4

Arrows Words 5

Arrows Words 6

Arrows Words 7

Arrows Words 8

Arrows Words 9

Arrows Words 10

Arrows Words 11

Arrows Words 12

ANSWERS

ANSWERS

ANSWERS

ANSWERS

Arrows Words 49

Arrows Words 50

Arrows Words 51

Arrows Words 52

Arrows Words 53

Arrows Words 54

Arrows Words 55

Arrows Words 56

Arrows Words 57

Arrows Words 58

Arrows Words 59

Arrows Words 60

List of the words used in the games

3

ACT
ADD
AGE
AGO
AIR
ALL
AND
ANY
ARM
ART
ASK
BAD
BAG
BAR
BAT
BED
BIG
BIT
BOX
BOY
BUS
BUT
BUY
CAN
CAR
CAT
COW
CRY
CUT
DAD
DAY
DIE
DOG
DRY
EAR
EAT
EGG
END
EYE
FAR
FAT
FEW
FIG
FIT
FLY
FOR
FUN
GAS
GET
GUN
GUY
HAT
HER
HIM
HIS
HIT
HOT
HOW
ICE
INN
JOB
JOY
KEY
LAW
LAY
LEG
LET
LIE
LOG
LOT
LOW
MAN
MAP
MAY
MIX
NEW
NOR
NOW
OFF
OIL
OLD
OUR
OUT
OWN
PAY
PUT
RED
ROW
RUB
RUN
SAW
SAY
SEA
SEE
SET
SEX
SHE
SIT
SIX
SKY
SON
SUN
TAX
TEN
THE
TIE
TOO
TOP
TRY
TWO
USE
WAR
WHO
WHY
WIN
YES
YET
YOU

4

ABLE
ALOT
ALSO
AREA
ARMS
ATOM
BABY
BACK
BALL
BAND
BANK
BASE
BEAR
BEAT
BELL
BEST
BILL
BIRD
BLOW
BLUE
BOAT
BODY
BONE
BOOK
BORN
BOTH
BURN
CALL
CAMP
CARD
CARE
CASE
CELL
CENT
COAT
COOK
COPY
CORN
COST
CROP
DARK
DEAD
DEAL
DEAR
DEEP
DICE
DIET
DOOR
DOWN
DRAW
DROP
EACH
EASE
EAST
EASY
EDGE
ELSE
EVEN
EVER
FACE
FACT
FAIL
FAIR
FALL
FARM

List of the words used in the games

FEAR	HOME	MEAN	PLUG	SAVE	TAIL
FEED	HOUR	MEAT	POEM	SEAT	TAKE
FEEL	HUGE	MENU	POOR	SEED	TALE
FEET	IDEA	MILE	PORT	SEEM	TALK
FISH	INCH	MISS	POSE	SELF	TALL
FLAT	IRON	MORE	POST	SEND	TASK
FOOT	JUMP	MOST	PUSH	SHIP	TEAM
FOUR	KEEP	MUCH	RACE	SHOE	TERM
FREE	KILL	NAME	RAIL	SHOP	TEST
FROM	KIND	NEAR	RAIN	SHOW	THAN
GAME	KING	NECK	RATE	SIDE	THAT
GIRL	KNOW	NEED	READ	SIGN	THEM
GIVE	LADY	NEXT	REAL	SITE	THEN
GLAD	LAKE	NICE	REST	SIZE	THEY
GOAL	LAND	NINE	RICH	SKIN	THUS
GOLD	LAST	NOON	RIDE	SLIP	TIME
GOOD	LATE	NOSE	RISE	SLOW	TINY
GRAY	LEAD	NOTE	RISK	SNOW	TONE
GROW	LEFT	NOUN	ROAD	SOFT	TOOL
HAIR	LESS	ONCE	ROCK	SOIL	TOWN
HALF	LIKE	ONLY	ROLE	SOME	TREE
HAND	LINE	OPEN	ROLL	SOON	TRIP
HARD	LIST	OVER	ROOM	SORT	TRUE
HAVE	LIVE	PAGE	ROOT	SPOT	TUBE
HEAD	LOSE	PAIN	ROPE	STAR	TYPE
HEAR	LOSS	PART	RULE	STAY	UNIT
HEAT	LOUD	PAST	SAFE	STEP	VARY
HELP	MAIN	PATH	SAIL	STOP	VERB
HERE	MANY	PICK	SALT	SUIT	VERY
HOLD	MARK	PLAN	SAME	SURE	VIEW
HOLE	MASS	PLAY	SAND	SWIM	VOTE

List of the words used in the games

WAIT	ARMED	CROSS	GUIDE	ORDER	SERVE
WALK	AVOID	DANCE	HAPPY	ORGAN	SEVEN
WALL	BASIC	DEATH	HEART	OTHER	SHAKE
WANT	BEGIN	DREAM	HEAVY	OWNER	SHARP
WARM	BLACK	DRESS	HOBBY	PAINT	SHEET
WEAR	BLOCK	DRINK	HORSE	PAPER	SHINE
WEEK	BOARD	EARLY	HOUSE	PEACE	SHOOT
WHAT	BREAD	EARTH	LARGE	PHONE	SIGHT
WHEN	BRING	EIGHT	LAUGH	PIECE	SINCE
WIDE	BROWN	ENEMY	LEARN	PITCH	SLAVE
WORD	BUILD	ENTER	LEAST	PLACE	SLEEP
WORK	CARRY	EQUAL	LEAVE	PLAIN	SMALL
YARD	CATCH	EVENT	LEVEL	PLANE	SMELL
YEAH	CAUSE	EVERY	LOCAL	PLANT	SOLVE
YEAR	CHAIR	EXACT	MATCH	POINT	SOUTH
YOUR	CHART	EXIST	METAL	POWER	SPACE
	CHECK	FALSE	MODEL	PRESS	SPEAK
5	CHIEF	FAVOR	MONEY	QUART	SPEED
ABOUT	CHORD	FIELD	MONTH	QUICK	SPELL
ABOVE	CLASS	FINAL	MOUNT	RADIO	SPEND
ADMIT	CLEAR	FIRST	MOVIE	RAISE	SPORT
ADULT	CLIMB	FLOOR	MUSIC	RANGE	STAFF
AFTER	CLOCK	FRESH	NEVER	REACH	STAIN
AGAIN	CLOSE	FRONT	NIGHT	READY	STAND
AGENT	CLOUD	GLASS	NOISE	REPLY	START
AGREE	COACH	GRAND	NORTH	RIGHT	STATE
ALLOW	COAST	GRASS	OCCUR	RIVER	STEAM
AMONG	COLOR	GREAT	OCEAN	ROUND	STEEL
ANGER	COURT	GREEN	OFFER	SCALE	STICK
APPLE	COVER	GROUP	OFTEN	SCENE	STILL
APPLY		GUESS		SCORE	STOCK

List of the words used in the games

STONE	WATER	ATTACK	DECIDE	IMPACT
STORE	WHEEL	AUTHOR	DEGREE	INSECT
STORY	WHERE	BACKUP	DESERT	INVENT
STUDY	WHICH	BEAUTY	DESIGN	ISLAND
TABLE	WOMAN	BEFORE	DETAIL	LATEST
TEACH	WOMEN	BEHIND	DIFFER	LAWYER
THANK	WORLD	BETTER	DINNER	LENGTH
THEIR	WORRY	BITTER	DOCTOR	LIKELY
THERE	WRONG	BRANCH	DOLLAR	LISTEN
THICK	YOUNG	BRIGHT	DOUBLE	LITTLE
THING		BUDGET	DURING	MAGNET
THIRD		CAMERA	EFFECT	MANAGE
THREE	6	CAREER	EFFORT	MATTER
THROW	ABJECT	CENTER	EITHER	MELODY
TODAY	ACCEPT	CHANCE	ENERGY	METHOD
TOTAL	ACTION	CHANGE	ENGINE	MODERN
TOUCH	AFFECT	CHARGE	ENOUGH	MOMENT
TOUGH	AFRAID	CHOICE	EXCITE	NATION
TRACK	AGENCY	CHOOSE	EXPECT	NATURE
TRADE	ALMOST	CHURCH	EXPERT	NOTICE
TRAIN	ALWAYS	CIRCLE	FIGURE	NUMBER
TREAT	AMOUNT	CLOTHE	FOLDER	OFFICE
TRUTH	ANIMAL	COLONY	FOLLOW	OPTION
UNDER	ANSWER	CORNER	FRIEND	OTHERS
UNTIL	APPEAR	COUPLE	GARDEN	OXYGEN
USUAL	AROUND	COURSE	GATHER	PARENT
VALUE	ARRIVE	CREASE	GOSPEL	PEOPLE
VISIT	ARTIST	CREATE	GROUND	PERIOD
VOICE	ASSUME	DANGER	HAPPEN	PERMIT
VOWEL	ASWELL	DECADE	HEALTH	PERSON

List of the words used in the games

PHRASE	STRONG	BEDROOM	FREEZER	PROBLEM
PLANET	SUFFIX	BELIEVE	GENERAL	PROCESS
PRETTY	SUPPLY	BETWEEN	HIMSELF	PRODUCT
RATHER	SYMBOL	BILLION	HISTORY	PROGRAM
REASON	SYSTEM	BLANKET	HUNDRED	QUALITY
RECENT	TENDER	BROTHER	IMAGINE	REALITY
RECORD	THEORY	CERTAIN	IMPROVE	RECEIVE
REDUCE	THOUGH	CHOPPED	INCLUDE	REFLECT
REGION	THREAT	COMPANY	INSTANT	REMOVED
REMOVE	TICKET	CONCERN	MACHINE	SCIENCE
REPEAT	TOWARD	CONNECT	MEASURE	SECTION
REPORT	TWENTY	CONTAIN	MENTION	SERIOUS
RESULT	UNIQUE	CONTROL	MESSAGE	SEVERAL
RETURN	VALLEY	COOKING	MILLION	SHAMPOO
SCHOOL	WEAPON	COUNTRY	NATURAL	SIMILAR
SEARCH	WEIGHT	DESPITE	NETWORK	SPECIAL
SEASON	WONDER	DEVELOP	NOTHING	STATION
SECOND	WRITER	DISCUSS	NUMERAL	STRANGE
SELECT	YELLOW	DISEASE	OBSERVE	STRETCH
SENIOR		ECONOMY	OFFICER	STUDENT
SERIES	7	ELEMENT	OPERATE	SUBJECT
SIMPLE	ACCOUNT	ELEVATE	PARTNER	SUPPORT
SINGLE	ADDRESS	EVENING	PATIENT	SURFACE
SOCIAL	AGAINST	EXAMPLE	PATTERN	TEACHER
SPEECH	ALREADY	FASHION	PERHAPS	THOUGHT
SPREAD	ARRIVAL	FEDERAL	POPULAR	THROUGH
STREAM	ARTICLE	FEELING	POSTMAN	TOWARDS
STREET	AVOCADO	FINALLY	PREPARE	TRAINEE
STRING	AWESOME	FINANCE	PRESENT	VARIOUS
STROKE	BECAUSE	FITNESS	PRIVATE	VILLAGE

List of the words used in the games

WARNING
WEATHER
WEDDING

8
ACTIVITY
ACTUALLY
AMERICAN
APPROACH
APTITUDE
BEHAVIOR
BLACKOUT
BUSINESS
CAMPAIGN
CARRYOUT
CONSIDER
CONTINUE
CULTURAL
CUSTOMER
DESCRIBE
DIVISION
ELECTION
ELECTRIC
EVIDENCE
EXERCISE
FRACTION
HOSPITAL
INCREASE
INDICATE
INDUSTRY

INTEREST
LANGUAGE
LENGTHEN
MAGAZINE
MATERIAL
MILITARY
MOLECULE
MOUNTAIN
MOVEMENT
NATIONAL
NEIGHBOR
NOTEBOOK
OBLIGATE
OFFICIAL
OPPOSITE
ORIGINAL
PHYSICAL
PLEASANT
PRACTICE
PRESSURE
PROBABLE
PROBABLY
QUOTIENT
RECENTLY
RELATIVE
RESEARCH
RESOURCE
SECURITY
SENTENCE
SHOULDER

STRAIGHT
STRATEGY
SURPRISE
SYLLABLE
THOUSAND
TOGETHER
TRAINING
TRIANGLE

9
ADVANTAGE
AGREEMENT
AUTHORITY
BEAUTIFUL
CANDIDATE
CHALLENGE
CHARACTER
CONSONANT
DIFFERENT
DIRECTION
EDUCATION
EQUIPMENT
ESTABLISH
FIRSTNAME
FOREIGNER
KNOWLEDGE
NECESSARY
NEWSPAPER
PARAGRAPH
PRESIDENT

PROFESSOR
REPRESENT
RIGHTHERE
SITUATION
SOMETIMES
STRUCTURE
SUBSTANCE

10
DICTIONARY
DIFFICULTY
EMPLOYMENT
ESPECIALLY
GENERATION
INSTRUMENT
PARTICULAR
POPULATION
REPUBLICAN
UNIVERSITY

11
ACCORDINGTO
BLACKFRIDAY
ENVIRONMENT
INFORMATION
INSTITUTION
PERFORMANCE
TEMPERATURE

12
HEADQUARTERS
ORGANIZATION

PROFESSIONAL
RELATIONSHIP

13
INTERNATIONAL

14
ADMINISTRATION

Printed in France by Amazon
Brétigny-sur-Orge, FR